SELECTED POEMS

Also by Clive Wilmer

POETRY

The Dwelling-Place
Devotions
Of Earthly Paradise

TRANSLATIONS
(with George Gömöri)

Forced March:
Selected Poems of Miklós Radnóti

Night Song of the Personal Shadow:
Selected Poems of György Petri

EDITIONS

Thom Gunn:
The Occasions of Poetry

John Ruskin:
Unto this Last & Other Writings

Dante Gabriel Rossetti:
Selected Poems and Translations

William Morris:
News from Nowhere & Other Writings

INTERVIEWS

Poets Talking:
The 'Poet of the Month' Interviews from BBC Radio 3

CLIVE WILMER

Selected Poems
1965-1993

CARCANET

First published in 1995 by
Carcanet Press Limited
402-406 Corn Exchange Buildings
Manchester M4 3BY

A CIP catalogue record for this book
is available from the British Library
ISBN 1 85754 134 0

The publisher acknowledges financial assistance
from the Arts Council of England

Set in 10 pt Sabon by Bryan Williamson, Frome
Printed and bound in England by SRP Ltd, Exeter

Funded by
THE
ARTS
COUNCIL
OF ENGLAND

To Tamsin and Gabriel

We love best what is given us: no choices
Speak to us like our new-born babies' voices.

Children, if you have ever felt neglected,
Don't blame me. Blame the children I've selected.

Contents

Of Earthly Paradise (1992)

New Poems

Translations

Prefatory Note

It would not be quite true to say that this volume contains *all* the poems that I wish to keep – I am not without sentimentalities – but these are the poems on which I should wish to be judged. They are also in what I hope will be the final versions. I have introduced a few revisions here and there, almost all of them very minor; many of them restore versions earlier than those that appeared in print. I have also rectified a few slight errors.

I have taken the opportunity to revive four poems that, for various reasons, I left out of earlier volumes: 'The Long Climb', 'Two Cambridge Images' and 'A Plaque'. I have inserted these where they might have appeared in the books from which I omitted them.

I have also included some of my verse translations. Where these were originally integral to my collections, I have allowed them to stay where they were. More peripheral ones I have moved to a separate section, where they mingle with translations written for less personal reasons. The versions from Hungarian and Polish were written in collaboration with George Gömöri. I am enormously grateful to him for introducing me to so much remarkable work that would otherwise have been unavailable to me. The Hungarian poems are taken from our two books, *Forced March: Selected Poems of Miklós Radnóti* (Carcanet Press, 1979) and *Night Song of the Personal Shadow: Selected Poems of György Petri* (Bloodaxe Books, 1991). Lyubomir Nikolov's 'Scaling Carp' was translated in collaboration with the poet himself. The versions of Fernando Pessoa were written for the Pessoa Centenary issue of the magazine *Numbers*. Since I do not speak Portuguese, I wrote them with the help of cribs and dictionaries; I am therefore grateful to the scholar and translator Peter Rickard for giving me linguistic help and literary advice at the final stage.

During the composition of the new poems, I was awarded an Authors' Foundation grant. My thanks to the judges, the Foundation and the Society of Authors, who administer these awards.

Some of the uncollected items have appeared in the following periodicals: *Hungarian Quarterly, New Poetry Quarterly, Numbers, PN Review, Portcullis, Southern Review, Spectator, TLS*. I am grateful to the relevant editors.

CLIVE WILMER

The Dwelling-Place

(1977)

The Dedication

E.W., 1882-1948

It was your room they moved me to
  (I, not yet four the year you died,
  Not grasping how I might have cried),
Dear Father, whom I hardly knew;

And your great, polished chest-of-drawers
  Was all that I inherited
  Besides: it loomed above my bed:
Dark in the wood-grain still there pours

In memory, vast, the gathered deep –
  Huge waves that surged, curded to foam
  (In the security of home),
And broke, as I sank into sleep.

Clearing those drawers out, grown to man,
  I came upon your photograph:
  It seemed a visual epitaph
To one I never thought, till then,

I'd loved or feared. Now time had blurred
  Your placid features, void of care,
  Who died, as if you had no heir,
Intestate: so on me conferred

No such authority as dressed,
  In my conception, all your acts;
  Mere rooms to occupy as facts –
No freehold rightfully possessed.

Moreover, childish hands, untaught
  In every art but innocence,
  Had scribbled into radiance
The aspect which the lens had caught

And overlaid its sepia hue –
  Your clothes now black and gold, your face
  Crimson, the sky (your dwelling-place)
Empty but touched with purest blue –

As if a fatherless naïf,
    Dreaming a different element,
    Within the oval frame had meant
To translate his confused belief

Into pictorial commentary:
    This was the palimpsest I'd scrawled
    Glimpsing a King, beyond my world,
Who governed from across the sea.

Your power you held but to resign –
    A rationally gentle reign;
    I see you smiling, mild again,
Whose failing life engendered mine;

And through my childhood dreams, that face
    Taught what a child could never see:
    That I must never hope to be
The master of my dwelling-place.

1975

The Exile

I threw up watchtowers taller than my need
With bare walls the enemy could not scale,
I wrenched stone from the near country-side
And built my city on the highest hill;
    Over the land I scarred I reared
Impenetrable the walls and citadel.

Then to approach the city from afar
All you could see was soaring, there was such peace
Knowing the city mine I lay secure.
My own, one night, woke me – every face
    A jutting rock relief in glare,
The torchlight that illumined new distress.

16

They lit me into darkness. The harsh sun
– My understanding dazzled when it dawned –
Disclosed me vulnerable. I stumbled on,
Till blown, a sterile seed, by years like wind
    Indifferent guidance, I am set down
Among familiar stone in a changed land.

Now it is only details I perceive:
The towers lopped, stone interspersed with weed
In patches; a deeper speckling seems to give
Form to the complex of decay, but is fled
    With a lizard flicker. Poppies revive,
In the wall they spatter, spectres of old blood.

The Invalid Storyteller

Lace, we remember, faded lace
To filter light and veil the panes
    Against the external day.
The light was intermeshed with lace
Upon the wall, fastidious,
In patterns subtle as decay
    And intricate as pain:
Like pinks and greens on carcasses,
Like wrinkles on an old man's face.

Beyond our reach, above the veil
Where knowledge knit with pain and death
    Shimmered, the sun's rays
Burst through the panes and cast a pale
Rectangular frieze upon the wall,
Whose colours told of summer days,
    Whose pallor told of death;
Where he could watch what he recalled
Advancing, as he told each tale.

The Sparking of the Forge

Stiffened and shrunk by age my grandfather
Leans forward now, confined within his chair,
Straining to raise a finger to point back
Over his shoulder, scarcely able to look
Over his shoulder through the darkening window
At the road behind him and before me where

The mailcoach ran just seventy years ago –
He suddenly tells me, reaching to capture one
Glimpse of the road where memory finds its form
And in whose lamps so many memories burn:
The armed guard in the rear, behind bars –
Changing the horses at the road's end inn –

And where we buy his tobacco every day
Was once a blacksmith's forge. I watch him stare
Into the crumbling coal and feel the blaze
Flare in the ancient forge and his childhood-eyes;
And whether the shoes were hammered on red-hot
Uncertain now, he recollects their glare.

His words uncertain now I watch him see
Bright in his mind the sparking of the forge,
The monstrous anvil and the sizzling steel,
The raising of the hammer high to feel
What once he had of muscle in his arm,
The hammer's beat sounding his deepest urge.

Each time recalled another fragment lost,
Still his past steps back – with broken breath –
Continuous in a stream of memories.
I pick up only broken images:
Confined by time, as he is by his age,
My own time's loss I find in his lost youth.

An old man's death becomes a young man's rage;
I seize the coal-tongs; now the blacksmith's clamp
Shadows my tiny room with smouldering giants,
An arm is raised to fall which, falling, hurls
Hammer-blows forward rung with resonance;
And, shod with steel now, hear the hard hoof stamp.

East Anglian Churchyard

for Robert Wells

The land – low-lying, the fen drained –
still partakes of the flood, and the soil
of this green graveyard still has the swell,
the broken swell, of a calm sea, beneath which
graves are submerged.

And this church – dateless, its wall at a lean
and no tower – is a beached ship,
perhaps of northern pirates who having no more
rich coastal abbeys to fire, settling,
passed from the blue.

From the deep half-salvaged, there is one tombstone
rears above the surface where leaf-light swims
in the shade of an oak-tree, ageless, ivied –
the stone entwined by the same ivy, its name
blotted by moss.

Beside recent deaths, no other stone
in sight – though here and there, a vague swell
covers a forgotten life. This
particular spot in the shade, he must have
chosen for memory.

The Portrait

Born in India where the sun glared
at the stoical English; his father's lip
stiff under the huge moustache, knit
with grizzled whiskers over the stiff
gilding of his red coat's collar; his mother,
haughty, decked in imperial silks,
her boned collar; the father's hands
so massive, sinewed and scarred and no
soft lulling at the mother's breast:
a Victorian childhood, steel grey.

Sent back home to England: for hard
study and games under threat of the birch,
the runs before breakfast, the cold baths:
to make a man of him.
                      And in manhood
(before the Depression's grime, old age
and death) unfit for the Great War, tall
in Edwardian grey, a slight physique;
and his pale, melancholy, liberal eyes
fade from the picture looked at two wars past
by his son, who has no children, and remembers.

Victorian Gothic

for Dick Davis

Blackened walls: a Gothic height
Crouches and does not soar, locked
To the earth like slabs of outcrop stone
That touch no God; they imitate

Monoliths of the moors. Smokebound
Maze of streets in a northern town,
Low-skied misted marshland: ghosts
Haunt him, a grave imagination.

Mist merged with industrial smoke
Where the ghosts swim:
Their scrawny bodies topped with blackened heads
Like those that peer through jungle leaves.

Manufacturers, poets, moralists, colonisers, all
Engendered empires of despair
Built on blackness in the grey air.

What does the grey stone mask? Such battlements
Attest obscure defence.
                          His mind draws
Close to its melancholy: as
In dank winter to the heaped log-fire
Of a Saxon hall, beyond whose walls
What lurks in greyness?

Castles from dark days his reason
Girdles like siege but preserves,
Long years of siege that constitute defence;
Renascence ghosts, dark blood
Steams on the axe – industrial fumes
Dry the blood of the starved worker – marshland
Dank at sunset the sky bleeds
Pillarbox red.

The Ruined Abbey

And now the wind rushes through grassy aisles,
And over the massy columns the sky arches.

The monks who built it
Were acquainted with stone and silence.
Knowing the grandeur and endurance
Of isolated winter oaks, of rock,
And the hard rhythms of moors,
They retired here and reared it
From the crust of the north, moulding this form
Around their core of silence.

Their minds were landscaped.
Not with summer gardens that give sense ease
Nor beaches that lull questionings to a doze.
Their landscapes asserted agonies that
Probed them to the nerve;
The hardness of rock and the stream's ice
Formed a resistance they learned to resist,
To subdue, till it yielded
To silent movements of joy –
To the penetrating warmth of a mellow sun,
Its venerable eye.

The streams locked by ice,
The rocks, and the edged wind
Resisted the cowled will to define.
But resistance tautened questionings whose sinew
Shaped understandings.
The moor's silence snowed meanings,
And they knew that, while ice melts or cracks, they
Could endure like the rocks.

And so from the stone of landscaped minds, they fashioned
A form for those meanings, a form
That arched over meaningful air.
According to their time they shaped it
With massive grace.
And in the face of evil, weathers and decay
Its essence constant in the shiftings of ages.

And now the wind rushes through the grassy aisles,
And over the massy columns the sky arches.

In ruin, the form remains;
When the form falls, there is stone;
Stone crumbled, there is still
The dust, dust, and a silence
The centuries bow to – a silence
Lapped by the speechless howl of winds.

Yorkshire, the West Riding, 1965

The Long Climb

not that run
into the candled darkness
with light enough for you not
to see your sins by —
light enough
to daze you with a beauty that does not speak
of the long struggle, but rather

climbing winding stairs
to the top of an ancient tower, so tall
it seems to have no end —
   and less light there, the turning
in narrowest confines, and
asperity of cold stone —

where the small light calls to a search
for the more there may be, the climb no
perversely tortuous
fascination lit with glimmers —
   abrasion, this is it, you can
crack your skull in the dark on stone, graze
blood-points from the skin, fall even
in sprawled confusion, but this

is where life touches — where blood
run to the head, the heart
beats to its peril — and there is for you
(unable to see round corners)
no end
to the long climb

unless you should reach the top —
from the start your aim though lost
often enough
when your only thought was climbing —
and from it see

spread out before you the whole of it

when the eye goes journeys
league upon league over land
in the clear sun, light that

hardens edges yet
infuses all with itself
is strong, this

(if at all you reach it
if it be there)
this is the vision

Florence, 1968

The Well

All day to gaze down into a well
as into yourself – as through self
to the blue sky fringed with green

of the world; and at length,
through a tunnelled forest of fronds that grow
from the mossy walls, to perceive

only your own face against the sky,
eyes glazed in contemplation, staring back
through a forest: is at large

to behold and desire to behold
– through foliage and from beyond darkness –
always, as in a well, meeting your stare,

your own face afloat on the surface,
with your thoughts bubbling from the deep spring
and your voice, reverberant, echoing response;

and to forget how without it
there is only the old perspective into endless dark
with silence at the source.

The Rector

Naturalist, poet, priest (1753-1830)

Privation for the poor
    Was want of a shared soul,
And hungry intellect was stripped
    Of serviceable role,

When in that partial Eden
    The guardian of the Word
Had died, their pastor, who had named
    The creatures of the Lord.

For the Word formed his thought,
    His task to make collation
Of scripture with what quickened it,
    The other book, creation;

And to the inward order
    Thus answered, testify
In prose whose measured harmony
    Compassed the butterfly;

Or verse that singled out
    Familiar things: which could –
From prospect near or far – reveal,
    In them, a primal good:

The truth he sought. Such fortune!
    For love could move the search,
Till all that his attention held
    Attended on his church

And drew toward the walls
Thick creepers still embrace,
Where chastened by the sombre yew
Light haunts his resting-place.

There once, a kind of pilgrim,
I thought how sad and mean
(Being shrunken to that yard and grove)
Was his once-fair demesne

And seeing the grave stones
As fragments of his store,
I felt – from hedgerow, evening air
And stream – his spirit soar

But met him in my own
Unsanctuaried spirit
Among the stones of an estate
I never shall inherit.

Arthur Dead

Terror stalks this land where once King Arthur
    Ruled with virtue steeped in vision;
Now in restless vigil his knights quest, their impulse
    Dark obsession.

Yet those few, who halting at the wayside
    Kneel to victims of the terror,
Salvage thus, from desolation which they ride in,
    Love and honour.

In Malignant Times

Within this hollow vault here rests the frame
Of that high soul wch late inform'd the same
Torn from the service of the state in's prime
By a Disease malignant as the time
Who's life and death designd no other end,
Than to serve God his Country & his friend
Who when Ambytyon Tyrany & Pride
Conquer'd the Age, Conquer'd Hymself & dyd

Epitaph for James Rivers (d. 1641),
in the Priory Church of St Bartholomew-
the-Great, Smithfield

1. IN TIME OF CIVIL WAR

A doctor: for the time's disease
He knew no cure: though he could ease
This mind's unrest, that body's pain.
The makeshift home where he was sane
Housed tranquil dignity, that bore
Sober mistrust for holy war.

The war he died in was not his:
Between two equal enemies
He chose to work withdrawn. But when
Ordered to sacrifice those men –
Patients and friends – who shared his home,
He chose to fight the war, alone.

Scorning promiscuous rhetoric,
With chaste formality he spoke:
The abstract words of his defence
Were tempered by experience,
No more: beyond that point he chose
The silence of secure repose.

2. ON A LUTHERAN PASTOR WHO PREACHED AGAINST HITLER

Ein feste Burg ist unser Gott

The time's demon had all but quelled
The faith he taught, to which he held
In doubt and hope. So he withdrew
To preach a version of the true:
Exiled within reality
To mediate lost sanctity.

When a Black Death of the spirit broke
Over Europe in blood and smoke
And silence, his truth named as fact
What lucid empiricism lacked
Scope to envisage. A stronghold still
For him, his faith embraced the real.

His speech was action. The long quest
Of Europe's centuries seems compressed
Behind those words: which yet contain
In their calm voice his insight's pain;
Which drove hysteria and pride
Beyond the clearing where he died.

Of Epitaphs

Not at peace with itself, in troubled times,
A divided mind might find sanctuary
Where yew-trees shade a field of scattered tombs
Subsidence tilts – or where an ambulatory,
Chill cavern of hewn stone, with grace recalls
Strife-proven virtue upon marble scrolls.

Might find, reposed in language that attests
To lives by death perfected, homages
Acclaiming perfect lives and certain rests.
Mere word and stone. Enduring images
Of what a culture trusted could be true
Or how such faith refracts what mortals do.

We though, our good a makeshift, may conceive
Of moral symmetry as mere *simplesse*
Or artifice – since we are bound to live
Poised between thought and what our thoughts address.
We, sceptics in our wisdom, miss their vice
Whose virtue, being substantial, could suffice.

Likeness

In John the Pisan's statue at Siena
Of the wolf suckling Romulus and Remus,
In the anxious eyes and searching nose – the low
Thrust of her gaunt head from the prominent spine,

I see my own dog: she, though sweetly pampered,
Looked drained and scrawny when, still half a puppy,
With bleeding teats, she bowed beneath her instinct
To mother her first brood: I see this much

As he, the sculptor, must have seen the she-wolf
And every burden dour fate lays on us
In the bent head of a spurned mongrel bitch
Upon the streets of Pisa or Siena.

To the Undeceived

'...to play the game of energetic barbarism...
is, after all, a mental and moral impossibility.'
Borges, *Other Inquisitions*

You who invoke survival, and condemn
To ruin all the crumbling palaces
And shady temples, where I seek the dim
Outline of order; who trust, that there is

Sufficient order in the wilderness
To harbour man, that unhistoric air
May yield desolate words, that consciousness
Must be most lucid sunk in black despair;

You are the more deceived of us: the night
Of your dark souls inherits a desire
That burns in you, as it were for the sight
To wearied Romans of their world on fire.
What answer you are the oncoming hordes
You'd join, at length to fall on your own swords.

Padua

Two Inscriptions

1. THE GOLDSMITH

To stay anxiety I engrave this gold,
Shaping an amulet whose edges hold
A little space of order: where I find,
Suffused with light, a dwelling for the mind.

2. JACK IN THE GREEN

for a roof-boss in a Gothic cathedral

Four oak-leaves from the dark behind his face
Sprout through his grin, and to this sacred place
Restore the primal counter-architecture,
Where four ribs hold and the head seals the structure.

Sanctuary

Torcello Cathedral

On the massive grey stone shutters (by stone rings
Hinged to the Roman windows of the church walls)
Are scars that might be some wedged archaic script –
Through time obscured, through history part-deciphered.

Brooding on these, we conjure a day of trouble
When a mudflat, where grass grows amid brackish fens,
Grew from the mist, a blurred hope, barely risen
From the grey, tideless sleep of the lagoon.

For them though, a clear space, between fear and the sea:
For – the last walls of their larger fortress, Empire,
Fallen to Northern barbarians, to the Lombards –
They had fled to sea: to build their hopes on sand.

There from the crude substance of memories and images
And marble salvaged from the waste that was once their home,
They hewed a temple, draining the land around it:
Sowed crops there, bred beasts, drew fish from the sea.

And raised a high tower reaching above the mist,
Bell-tower and watch-tower, over the sea's languor:
And marine-dull chimes from the bell that called to prayer
Would call to safety women children and cattle

Into the fortress of their sanctity.
Then doors were barred and the slabs rolled over the windows
To bear their silent witness to Eastern arrows,
And the men went out to confront their older adversary:

Not purgers of decadence – the indifferent offspring
Of history, whose molten rush is cast in words –
But immemorial, grey ghost-marauders
That broke on the shore, grey spume of the ancient sea.

The Disenchanted

On a painting by Atkinson Grimshaw,
'Liverpool Quay by Moonlight', 1887.

Riding at anchor ships from the New World,
Cargo-less now, sway, as in a trance;
Their lights float on a mist, their sails are furled;
They have disembarked both energy and distance.

Fated by deep unrest to haunt the quay
Aimless pilgrims, lit by the blear gaslight,
Emerge from haze, withdrawn in reverie:
     Exiles from day and night.

And at shop-windows they become transparent
To golden light that charms the brazen riches
There on display, before which they lament –
     As at vain reliquaries

That hold dead sanctity. They stare at distance
Imported by a manufactured world
To allure their wasting energy and substance
     By turning all to gold.

Bewitched but disenchanted lords they are,
Of a legendary treasure long since dispossessed,
Who drift with the dissolving atmosphere –
     Dim shades of the lost.

Only the lamp on a black, advancing coach
– Unearthly green! – can focus in reflection,
Composing all you see as you approach:
Light of the mind it stays from desolation.

Bird-Watcher

It returns to the same nest. The watcher lies
Beneath spring brushwood to await its coming –
At watch so long he dreams himself becoming
Less than himself and more, the landscape's eyes.

Though far beyond his eyes, beyond the range
Of field-glasses, he knows it breaks no bonds:
Its instinct to his knowledge corresponds,
Riding the current of the season's change.

What is there in a small bird's blood that learns
To plot its course by sun and stars, being drawn
Yearly toward a lost, remembered dawn?
The watcher broods on this. The bird returns.

And all its colours flash where he attends:
A deep blue mantling rust and white. It sings
Caged in his retina; then, on curving wings,
Veers off to vanish where the human ends.

Saxon Buckle

in the Sutton Hoo treasure

His inlaid gold hoards light:
A gleaming thicket to expel,
With intricacy worked by skill,
The encroaching forest night
Where monsters and his fear dwell.

Gold forest tangles twined by will
Become a knot that closes in
The wild beasts that begin
Beyond his habitation.
An object for his contemplation,

From which three rivets gaze:
A beast's head forested within,
That clasps his swordbelt to his waist
By daylight, and before his eyes,
By hearthlight, stills unrest.

Devotions

(1982)

To my Wife

Love, these are shapes of nothing, but they took
Time from our love, and time can never give
Of its own self again; so take my book,
This witness to an absence where I live.

The Advent Carols

Aspiciens a longe

I look from afar. We stand in darkness.
A people in exile, shall we hear good news,
Who, toward midnight, in mid-winter, sing?

Sing words to call a light out of the darkness
To thaw dulled earth, to unfold her fairest bud;
Our song holds faith that the Word will be made flesh.

Now we bear candles eastward, bear them into
Inviolate dark the Word should occupy:
Light disembodied swells the sanctuary

Where an old dream is mimed, without conviction,
Over again. I look from afar. Our sung words
Are herald angels, and they announce his name,

But lay no fleshly mantle on the King,
The one Word. And yet, in the song's rising
Is rapture, and dayspring in the mind's dark:

For the one sanctuary, now, is the word not
Made flesh – though it is big with child, invaded
By the dumb world that was before it was.

Narcissus, Echo

Only reflection sanctifies,
For him, the beauty she holds dear.

She calls and calls to him, till all
The vacant world resounds with love.

My Great-Aunt, Nearing Death

Her narrow life has straitened to this room.
Arranged like a saint's corpse in a reliquary –
Hands clasped
Over her virgin womb –
Her body lies,
Trusting that soon the hand of love will find her.
Blind eyes,
Focused on all or nothing.

Her life has known naive gentility
Only and so one thought that that defined her.
Yet charity
(Her visitors bear witness),
Though she is poor, is in her daily gift –
So call it love.

Blind hands –
Ignorant both of passion and of harm,
Hands she can barely lift –
With gentleness, conferring calm,
Reach out to where my little children stand:
They who, like her, fear nothing,
Doubt no love.

On the Demolition of the 'Kite' District

Cambridge 1980

On the smashed hearthstone or the fallen lintel
Carve words to witness:
                            That men who called themselves
Conservatives, lying in their teeth, tore down
Good rooms, good walls of weathered brick, erasing
A wordless register of birth and death.

Il Palazzo Della Ragione

Passing the central Palace (called 'of Reason')
In Padua, daily I'd contemplate,
High on one wall among begrimed inscriptions,

Leaning as from a window, a gentleman
In Quattrocento costume – with a turban.
He smiles across distance, his hand raised in greeting.

Smiling as if at me, to bid me welcome
To a city, enlightened and humane,
Whose style I can neither touch nor imitate.

And though I would not say,
'This is a final wisdom,
As of Christ or the Buddha, on the Palace of Reason,'

Yet it seems he has a graciousness
Beyond our time to emulate,
Though one may celebrate.

That smile across the ages is intent
On courtesy. And nonetheless,
I suffer it as though it were contempt.

Pony and Boy

  the pony presses
its muzzle into the bark
  of the tree blindly
as my boy, across the stream
leaning towards it, gazes

Two Cambridge Images

1. THE MARKET-PLACE AT MIDNIGHT

No moon,
but lamp light.

The fountain dead,
planks fallen.

Row upon row, still,
of stalls:
crude boards roped across
trestles, and slack canvas.

2. MICHAELMAS TERM, 1964

On gleaming flagstones
cold rain falls
        Young men walk
above the stores of vintage
        to the library

1968, 1979

Beyond Recall

for Thom Gunn

Imprecision of the senses at midday:
stirred,
      having been struck
by the sharp bitter-sweet of a new wine
drunk in a clouded bar
                         – where
to nose and tongue came the tang
of pickled onions, of briny olives and, raw
to the back of the throat, the reek
of cheap cigar smoke.

                Light
on crude gems that define a haze.
They, once possessed, – though precious
beyond recall – remain his
alone
      who inclining toward the past
hears nightingales in the dark, yet never can
transcribe
        their fluid melodies.

from *Air and Earth*

MIGRANT

O Redwing,
with your slashed sleeves, with
your speckled breast, the livid
stripe on your brow –

how you must stand out
against
the Iceland tundra – white
or grey – as with a
stain of your warm blood;
yet here

accommodate yourself
to songthrush and mild lawn,
and to that snow
of the new season: may,
streaking the hawthorn hedge.

BESIDE THE AUTOBAHN

It is sunk deep, this
motorway

        And all along it,
where the rats and mice –
now vulnerable, since they
cannot undermine a
causeway through their territory –
must cross,
        there perch
on fence-posts, nothing moved,
these long-eared owls
who wait

As,
through millennia, owl
eyes have to the dusk become
enlightened:
even so those ears,
to patterings
beneath the passing traffic, are
attuned

AERIAL SONGS

i

from his high perch
Thrush
sings the morning, from

an aerial
upon a chimney-stack –
above
the abstract foliage.

More than a
plump, warm,
speckled, dust-brown
body – he's

a voice,
awakening the city
folk
to what
daily lost but eternal
hour of the incipient.

The tree he has alighted
on was neither
born nor dies: so he
recurs

ii

likewise, at dusk,
Blackbird his brother:
plumage
            losing
in the dark – his bright bill
sings
the sun to setting.

And the air is his!
                        For us,
            that song
articulates
the space that was
before towns were.
                        It heralds,
retrospectively,
                        the sunk
emergence of our dwellings
from the greenwood –
                        from the green
world, dark and other.

For his bill is golden,
though the wings are swart.

NATURAL SELECTION

At first sight, *house-martins*
I thought: for what
other bird, what passerine, would lodge
so? – then I saw
the sparrow, peering from
no nest but a dark cavity
beneath the eaves.
                        Splendid more
than is commonly ackowledged:
this one, male – with his
grey crown and black bib, not so
mousy as the female – pert
scavenger: always

I've admired them
who, of all winged things, are fittest
to adapt.
          The house-martins and
all the swallow-kind, who with grace arch
our thoroughfares, have blessed
time out of mind – with
is it trust? – our home walls where they
build their nests: a natural
benediction.
          But the sparrows, not
the offspring of a freehold
freely entered into, now breed
in a mousehole, thrive
on dereliction.

                    *

          It is our
improvidence that has made way
for a world fit for what
nature (we say) *selects*; and we,
when we speak so, become
the self-elect, standing outside
the world we must now leave
to the once-welcome sparrow
and the rat – to cranny-dwellers, all
whose empires (our unwilled
bequest) shall flourish
where we die.
          And a dead world
we shall leave – crumbling
brickwork, rotting
eaves and rafters, songless
wood: a world stripped
of its old glories, where every
edifice of man
or god is gutted and
laid waste.
          The eagles
are departing now; not us,
still less the martins, we
shall not be the survivors.

ON THE DEVIL'S DYKE

for Michael Vince

In the hedgerows
            along this walk
songbird nests abound; and –
            as my dog runs on
interpreting
            on air and earth
rank traces and warm lingerings that
her cold nose pursues
            ahead of me –
the birds flutter out and away;
and beasts of undergrowth and hedgerow,
            rabbit fox and weasel,
stir within the radius of her scenting
unseen mostly,
            though from time
to time
            ahead of us
a red or brown
            streaks
the crisp white of the chalk ridge, and passes
through the eye's enduring field
            of green
and brown-and-green
            bound
in the clasp of the arched blue.
            There the skylarks
our footfalls drive from the warm clench of
nestling in the grass
            appear and disappear,
become what is the
            audible extent
– beyond sight –
            of the sky.

*

46

One might as well
                be walking further south,
the chalk hills there, it could be
                the South Downs.
But no:
                this is a made place, here
in the deep bone and sanctum
                of the land
is stamped the signature,
                the *homo fecit*,
of those who dug what we
                still call,
as the feared Norsemen did,
                a *dyke* –
no Saxon *ditch* (where a tramp
                might bed down).

                *

Defence
                was what they had in mind
who with this causeway
                bridged the fen to protect
their landward flank and so
                insulate a territory
plants birds and beasts
                ignore. And though you pass
from time to time
                into some tangled hedge,
are drawn into
                – enmeshed in, even –
green of the earth's making,
                yet you emerge
out on the bare ridge-way
                and, across the trench,
survey
                the furrowed ploughland in retreat,
envisage
                the advance of bristling armies
held
                in your long watch.

                *

47

A spring day
        and I lie back
on the full flank of the earth,
        the sloped wall of the bulwark.
I am weight, borne by what
        holds me down –
as the larks
        rise, till they are
out of range and
        the blank sky is all
the eye beholds,
        the heart and ear
tugged
        by a lilt and stagger that ascend
beyond perceiving: air,
        their scope of territory, their
earthly dwelling.

        Listen!
sing the larks
        down to me: you,
a man, live in a place. More,
        in a palimpsest of places:
landscape   history   creed   the word.
Through us you may infer those
        other worlds your map
and composite of places must at best
imply.
        Worlds often glimpsed
beyond your earthworks, ramparts, palisades.

        East Anglia

The Natural History of the Rook

The rooks are Gothick which have brought to mind
The naturalist Charles Waterton. He wrote
With care and indignation: an explorer:
A solitary who loved, above all creatures,
The birds of the air. When at his burial
A linnet sang out, fact gave rise to legend:
That the flotilla of black barges floating
His body to its lakeside grave had been
Escorted by long flights of birds in mourning.

Among them, rooks. From trees they pinnacle
Like symptoms of a fantasy, their humped
Black shapes unfold now, lifting, taking wing
To drape the sky with signs of lamentation.

No. Waterton – who one phantasmal night
Of gloom and tempest wrote in quietness,
Not fantasy not legend, but 'the history
Of the rook' – in the rook saw no gloom, would not
Submit to the 'blue devils' conjured up
By the November fogs but would combat them
With 'weapons of ornithology'.

                        He had –
'Having suffered himself and learned mercy' –
Laid his guns down, walled in his park and lake,
And made a pause in nature. There he watched,
Rejoicing in cacophony – explored
Downward
              toward a silence
                           undisturbed
The barn-owl winged its day through,
                               made a space
Where rooks alighted, their gregarious croak
In tune with an unheard polyphony
His prose, which does not venture to transcribe it,
Bespeaks. Of science and his own estate

He made himself
            a sanctuary
                        the mind
Questing could enter into, haunt in freedom,
And dwell in, freed of its own hauntings.

                                    Blithe
You must have been, Charles Waterton, to know
That the inequitable penal laws
Enforced by ignorance and sentiment
Against all 'pests and vermin', now repealed
By you, no longer warped the needful cycles
Of breeding and predation. Blithe you were
From your high perch to watch the darting turquoise
Spear the still pool, to hear the barn-own screech
No special doom to man, and see the rooks
Fly overhead in the dawn light to pass
Into the still-remote, unmediated
Variety of inhuman atmosphere.

Near Walsingham

Springs rise where saints have prayed,
        Tradition says;
    And tells of rivulets and wells
        Conceived of rumoured deities.

But streams would have obeyed
        No peremptory hand.
    Where water has already blessed the land
        Saints choose to pray.

Gods walk when glint and spade
        Strike, as it brims,
    A buried watercourse. And one dreams
        A cryptic meaning for the source:

Meaning which haunts the shade
　　That falls by bridge and ford
　Lodged in the thought and speech that hearken toward
　　The interminable

Tale given and not made
　　Or understood,
　Which haunts the place. What we might say
　　Of what it tells would speak of God.

Home

after Cesare Pavese

The lone man hearkens to the calm voice,
His features ajar – as if the draught
In his face were a breath, a friendly breath,
Returning, beyond belief, from time gone by.

The lone man hearkens to the ancient voice
His fathers throughout the ages have heard, clear
And composed, a voice that much like the green
Of the pools and hills deepens at evening.

The lone man knows a voice of shadow,
Caressing, and welling forth in the calm tones
Of a secret spring: intently, his eyes closed,
He drinks it down, and seems not to have it near him.

It is the voice that, one day, halted the father
Of his father, and each of the dead blood.
A woman's voice that whispers in secret
On the threshold of home, at the fall of darkness.

Homecoming

A Theme and Variations

1. MID-WINTER

The year goes out in wrath. And through the winter
Are scattered little days like cottages.
And lampless, hourless nights; and grey mornings,
Their indistinguishable images.

Summertime, autumn – time and season passing,
And brown death has seized on every fruit.
And new cold stars appear now in the darkness,
Unseen before, even from the ship's roof.

Pathless is every life. And every path
Bewildered. The end unknown. And whoso seeks
And finds a path finds that his utterance breaks
Off in sight of it, empty the hands he shakes.

2. A WINTER EVENING

When snow falls on pane and sill,
Long peals are borne on evening air;
The board is laid for many there
In a house provided well.

On their wanderings, several others
Come to the gate by dark ways.
Gold blossoms the tree of grace
Where cool sap in the earth gathers.

The wanderer quietly steps across
A threshold pain has turned to stone.
On the board glow bread and wine
In all the radiance of loss.

3. A THRESHOLD

You, centaury, o lesser star,
You birch, you fern, you oak:
Near me you stay as I go far...
Home, into your snare we walk.

Black on a bearded palm tree
Hangs cherry-laurel bunched like grapes.
I love, I hope, I believe...
The small date, split open, gapes.

A saying speaks – to whom? To itself: *Servir
Dieu est régner...*I can
Read it, I can – it is coming clear –
Get out of Me-no-unnerstan.

> *after Georg Heym, 'Mitte des Winters'*
> *Georg Trakl, 'Ein Winterabend'*
> *Paul Celan, 'Kermorvan'*

For the Fly-Leaf of a King James Bible

'*...in dürftiger Zeit*'
– Hölderlin

Now, in our needy time,
These words so flush with hope
Probe at the heart that aches toward the past
For the god not yet come.

Cadence and phrase and tone –
Derived by Jacobean
Divines from Tyndal and from Coverdale,
Refined – gain resonance.

A rhythm draws the mind
Through theirs to older scores:
Lollard and Saxon drafts; Latin behind,
A plainchant barely heard.

Then Greek, Hebrew, the first
Utterance of the word
Of one the many tongues have, differently,
Called 'God' with the same thirst.

This text – new from the press –
Already smelt of a time
Past, as if left to fust in cellars: earth-
begrimed, already foxed.

Now, in our needy time,
Virtue and beauty seem
In dark, like heady vintage, to mature:
Full-bodied and obscure.

Antiphonal Sonnets

Of John Taverner

John Taverner (c.1495-1545) was a composer of polyphonic church music. After his conversion to Protestantism, he seems to have renounced all musical activity and was employed by Thomas Cromwell in the spoliation of the monasteries. The first of these sonnets alludes to his respond Dum transisset sabbatum, *a setting of Mark xvi, 1-2. The second alludes to a letter from Taverner to Cromwell – 'according to your lordship's commandment the Rood was burned the seventh day'.*

1.

Suppose a man were dying and this sound
Washed over him: it would not be like sleep
But waking to set eyes for the first time
On the world, ours, yet other. For the sense
Of things would be the things themselves and words
Would gem the melismatic harmony
Rarely, articulating it. The mind –
In a language, the great mass of whose words
Are shattered into vagrant syllables
By gay polyphony – would edge towards

The scope of revelation, which is speechless.
Now, in the place of death, an angel sits
And speaks to three who mourn of interim,
Announces that the second day is done.

2.

This was the world: the word.
                                        Gratuitous day,
Stained by a red or a blue gaze, confined
By aspiring stone to space with no horizon:
Earthly things that composed an allegory
Which guessed at heaven. He cast given speech
Against the bossed and starry vaults, shattered it
To falling fragments, harmonies – a fertile
Resonance, as much like beauty as like that
It seemed at length to mask: in empty space
A simple disembodied word, the truth.
Then beauty was the hoofbeats in the nave,
The radiant shower of glass, a mace that knocked
Devotion from her pedestal, the flames
That burnt the rood in the broad light of day.

Gothic Polyphony

Space: tall, with no horizon. Plainsong scales
And vines the branched and foliating thrust
Of stone: to bloom polyphony: which fails
Against the ribbed vault's bossed and fretted crust.

To Nicholas Hawksmoor

When, as at Beverley Minster or All Souls,
You ape the Gothic, art is all façade.
Forms moulded of your substance, clear and hard,
Weigh with a Roman virtue. What controls

The impulse, at Christ Church, that would have soared
Through broken cornices to where a spire
Defined not form but anguish and desire,
Becomes your very theme at Castle Howard,

The Mausoleum. Private grief, though lost
In generalities of hope resigned,
There haunts the orders which the patient earth

Sustains for ruin. And something of the north
Troubles your cool sobriety of line
With aspiration and an edge of frost.

Venice

Salt-bleached marble, the green stain of seaweed.

A face the sea dismembers and remembers
Looks back at those who lean towards it, drowning
In admiration, in reflected glory.

Here man hath set his footprint on the waters.
We see the tides disperse it, see them relinquish
The white of marble and the green of seaweed.

A Woodland Scene

We think we detect a date: in the 1860s is it? – for that would fit. But no, it is merely a calligraphy of shadow and reflection, which leaves (overhanging it) have trailed across the stream in the foreground.

Then the painter's name, Maltby. This, we find, occurs in the standard reference book, but with different initials.

*

Watercolour, overlaid with bodycolour. 'Ruskinian,' a friend calls it. And so it is: in its anxious piety – in the endeavour to speak, crisply, of the transitory variegations of light on bark, or, where a bough has been shorn off, of light on pith; everywhere modified by the intervention of leaves, translucent or shadow-casting. Ruskinian, too, in the implied continuity of the given world with whatever a mesh of boughs and branches, contained within an arbitrary rectangle, can itself contain. Speaking, then, of the world at large, the picture expounds no painter, is devotional.

Encrusted with light, the leaves lose substance. Fretted with bodycolour, surface becomes depth. It is a sunny day. In our looking, we cool ourselves on the banks of a stream. We are somewhere in the depths of a wood. No people, no birds or beasts, and the world is still.

*

The craftsman who will restore it seems to care as much for frame, mount and glass as for the picture. 'Fine hand-made glass, that,' and how can he tell? He holds it horizontal to the eye and, see, light moves in waves across the lucid, tumbling surface, as if engendered by the glass itself. A still, translucent sea – becalmed – of greens and blues. Hung in its frame the glass, like the foliage it reserves for us, both absorbs and reflects, draws in and throws back such light as has entered the room. To the eye of the room-dweller, it interprets the light of the forest.

The frame is of oak. Dull with bituminous varnish and begrimed, until I stripped it with caustic. Then as the water dried, a rose-colour seemed to flush, elusively, in the damp grain of it. We shall preserve what we can of that, and the glass. But the mount has decayed, gone brown; and the card the picture was stuck on is pocked with mould

– 'Foxing,' says the craftsman: an impurity in the glue can cause it, or a dead fly. All this must be renewed.

*

It used to hang, I remember, in the dullest room of my parents' house, a room usually locked. Later, I rescued it from a windowless box-room. I have hung it near a window now, well in the light.

On occasion, the shade of the room blends with the shade of the woodland. Though often, where a treetrunk casts its shadow, day-light falls. Or the pool of imperfect glass becomes opaque with reflections that ripple above inferred profundity. From the other side of the room one begins to see (after long acquaintance) how the picture's uniformity of surface actually appears to tilt inwards, receding into distance through a region of paint where the light's greenish tints are touched with blue.

*

This blue is a threshold, the frame its gate or door. The wood is uninhabited. Let the picture's making and preserving restore to the woodland its absent spirits, recall to the hearthside our household gods.

The Parable of the Sower

*Stained glass in the Arts & Crafts style,
set in a medieval church*

I

The sower goes out to sow. His sense and form
Move only in a landscape of stained glass;
    The leads like ivy stems,
    Enmeshing, bind him in.
Outside, it is afternoon; inside, the sun
Irradiates a face in shadow – eyes

Inclined toward the earth
Crimsoning underfoot.
The glory round about and through his limbs
Is vision in excess of daily need,
Devotion in the work
Dispersed beyond the seed.

II

Victorian glass of eighteen ninety-seven,
Replacing the clear light in the west wall
In homage to a time
That built as if for ever.
The vision is of a vision that transfigured
Perspectives on the bare field; but with skill
The craftsman has contained,
Edged, the unearthly glow.
His observation accurate, the self
A blemish that his labour should efface,
Devotion to his craft
Speaks through the pictured face.

III

The sower does not see the field he sows.
He walks in rapture, but his eyes are glazed
With sorrow not his own,
That has no root in earth.
It is the craftsman's sorrow, for he gave
These paradisal colours to the earth
But when he looked on earth
He found an absence there.
Here wayside, thorn, good ground and stony ground
Are stained through with devotion, with his need
For things to mean – the word
Secreted in the seed.

The Peaceable Kingdom

for Tamsin and Gabriel

The wolf also shall dwell with the lamb, and the leopard shall lie down with the kid; and the calf and the young lion and the fatling together; and a little child shall lead them.

This morning, as I watch my son
   Play with a loved toy horse so small
   He need not fear it, I recall
His elder sister, not yet one,

Behind her cot-bars, turning to peep
   At me or, through the orbit of
   The animals that wheeled above
Her head, to watch enlarging sleep

Involve her tiny world – her laugh
   Hushed, and her babble, that addressed
   And answered it. Like things possessed,
Kangaroo, tiger and giraffe,

Pivoted from an elephant's
   Huge bulk, in genial caricature
   Grinning in disregard of her,
Went by her with a nod or prance.

Animals prowling through the air
   In cycles of pursuit, restrained
   From conflict by the space ordained
For harmony of movement: where

Else could the like be found but in
   A mind whose thoughts cannot efface
   With reasoning that longed-for place,
The garden of our origin?

– Which she had glimpsed, who thought and saw
   Nothing she could have known, a child
   Looking with trust upon the wild
Through distance unaccounted for.

Could this be that Arcadia
    Where 'inward laws that ruled the heart'
    Ruled nature, the Creator's art,
As well? Man the Artificer

Then was not: for his work presents,
    Apart from us, a world we stand
    Apart in and would understand;
He frees it from inconsequence,

Showing us – through attention paid
    To things the distances remove –
    That what is feared with reason, love
Need not renounce. Therefore he made

That mobile bestiary whose course
    My girl watched, and these animals
    Cluttered inside their farmyard walls,
Now, by my boy, who lifts a horse

As if he thought to elevate
    The mystery of flesh and blood,
    Priest-like, toward an unknown god,
To praise, and to propitiate.

Chinoiserie: The Porcelain Garden

Empty, flicked by a fingernail, the bowl
    Rings with the charm of vacancy. A girth
Of pure abstraction binds your world: a whole,
Void of anxiety and fond recall,
                    That stands free of the earth.

Revellers in blue glaze, your endless day
    Persuades you there is ground for careless mirth
That does not cloy. Nothing you do or say
Has death in it, as if your primal clay
                    Were not derived from earth.

The matter of your converse? Nothing said.
What profits you, what is your life there worth?
You smile. (Olympian...Mandarin...) The dead,
Even, could not be more disinterested
                    Or less ruled by the earth.

On the calm surface of the pool appears,
    Turned on its head, the world that gave you birth,
Denied you growth. And our world is to yours
What you are to the pool, whose rippling clears
                    Inconsequence from earth.

There you look on, and we glimpse paradise:
    A dream of beauty and a form of dearth.
One touch of pain, unmimed, might turn to vice
Your virtues. Beauty is gloss. Like constant ice,
                    Polar, yet of the earth.

Prayer for my Children

Te lucis ante terminum

Before the end of daylight, Lord
    Dweller in things, we pray you keep
    The custom of your watch when sleep
Annihilates you in our thought.

Untrouble us with dreams; the grim
    Phantasmagoria of the night
    Remove. In sleep the inward sight
Wakes and is powerless to condemn.

And, distant Father, if you hear
    The outcry of a sleeping child,
    Keep soul and body undefiled.
Then, in the absence, you are near.

Of Earthly Paradise

(1992)

To the Memory of my Mother
K.S.W. (1904-1985)

Alive, I could not write for you, who dead
Live in the words you planted in my head.

Invocation

Unanswering voice,
Sustainer,
Lady or Lord:
I have no choice
But to attend
Your silent word.

I think again
Of the first poet
Of my tongue:
Abandoning
The sweet, profane
Intoxication
Of plucked string
And exploit sung.

At your command
He sang creation.

He had withdrawn
To where
His silence was:
Where cattle stand
And, sleeping, moan,
Stamp, grumble, snort.

As in high places dawn
Will spring
Sudden from stone,
So from the dung
And bed-straw rose
His made thought.

Angel or Muse,
Because I do
Not hear your voice
Yet cannot choose
But speak, I pray

Let my words be
Such that they grow
From my silence
Answering you,
As they
Must answer me.

Two Versions of Caedmon

*This is the sense but not the selfsame order of the words which
he sang in his sleep: for songs, be they never so well made,
cannot be turned of one tongue into another, word for word,
without loss to their grace and worthiness.*

Bede's *Ecclesiastical History*

1. FROM THE LATIN

Now ought we all to sing
The author of what is –
To hymn his power, invoke his understanding,
Rehearse his actions, praise him –
Glorious Father:

Sing how, as he is God
Eternal, he became
And is the author of these miracles:
Who, for the sons of men,
Made heaven first

To roof their habitation:
Whereupon he, the one
Almighty guardian of the tribes of man,
Made and adorned that too:
It is the earth.

2. FROM THE OLD ENGLISH

Now should we hail   heaven's guardian,
Praise the Maker,   his might and thought,
The Father of glory,   his work: for he gave
To all wonders   one beginning –
           Everlasting Lord.
First he raised   a roof which is heaven
For the sons of men,   *sanctus artifex*;
And then in time,   everlasting Lord,
Mankind's guardian,   he made earth,
Made and adorned it,   almighty King.

Three Brueghel Paintings

The Massacre of the Innocents
The Conversion of St Paul
Hunters in the Snow

I

This is the world (the painter says)
Reduced by ice and snow, bone-bare.
    Then ride in mercenaries.
Armed to the teeth, they introduce
    Fear, panic and despair.
They'd trace a king. How can they know
           He is not here?

II

Where earth encounters heaven, cloud
Frays on the trees that spike the air.
    Ranks crumble to a crowd
Of stragglers. Some, bemused and dazed
    By light's intrusion, stare
At one the light has felled, who sees
           What is not there.

III

No myth informs this wintry view
Enhanced by no nostalgic care
    For skies of southern blue.
Skaters delight in circumstance
    Three hunters come to share,
Who slant against winds charged with snow
        From who knows where.

St Francis Preaching to the Birds

for Tamsin

Not angels these; although
Their melody and flight
Subsume the world, their wings
Substantiating light.

This man whom inwardness
And gracious thought have blessed,
Possessing nothing, knows
Both ear and eye possessed.

Their being crowds against
His gates of sense: to move
Into the mind, where language
Declares the movement love,

Though love is his, not theirs.
They, living beyond reach,
Indifferent to meaning,
Are made anew in speech.

The San Damiano Crucifix

which spoke to St Francis

A church about to fall.
The saint of poverty
Knelt in the church to pray,
Loving its poverty.

Flesh-tint and gold leaf
Hung there above him: a cross.
With bodily ears he heard
A voice speak from the cross

In pain, exhorting him
Repair my broken House.
Stone by stone he repaired
The body of that house:

For though the letter kills,
The spirit and the word
Move in the flesh alone.
So too, although the words

Spoken by painted wood
And answered in his work
May not be what we hear,
It is a speaking work.

The Coat of Many Colours

*Do not interpretations
belong to God?*

Joseph: Rich colour signifies deep inwardness.
          The bending sheaves, the sun's the moon's decline
          Are colours in this coat, my father's gift.
          Some bleed and blend. Others, like potentates,
          Stand out – see! – urgent and peremptory.

One of the   All his tall stories, dreams he calls them, stress
brothers: His own pre-eminence, its outward sign
             That coat he swaggers in... What but that gift
             Has he to show?... How his pretension grates,
             The smugness posing as authority!

Potiphar's   My mordant lust, no matter what he says,
wife: He woke in me. Now I dream his body's line,
             Its nervous thrust imprisoned, and the gift
             Of so reading desire his eye translates
             – Through cold reflection – heat to chastity.

Pharaoh: Amun, we are all, gaudy or poor our dress,
           Rich with an inwardness that seals us thine!
           I raise this man to greatness for a gift
           Beyond such wealth, since what his night creates
           His day interprets with lucidity.

Jacob: I dreamt you had not gone, though dreamt it less
         The nearer death I grew. O son of mine,
         Now I have found you, death shall be a gift,
         And dream and understanding the twin gates
         I pass through as I near reality.

Cattle Market

for Gabriel

Why brook'st thou, ignorant beast, subjection?
Why dost thou, bull and boar, so seelily
Dissemble weakness, and by one man's stroke die
Whose whole kind you might swallow and feed upon?

                                          Donne

Seely or silly?
                    Timorous beasts
Thwacked and buffeted into pens
Clamour against the world, although
The hands they suffer at are men's.
Terror masters them – it protests,
Seems to resist, then lets them go

Lambs to the slaughter, pigs, cows...
Men who stand and look on equate
Value with fleshly substance – price
The measure of it; and this they state
By way of nods and puckering brows.
Yet the whole place seems paradise

To one of them, who does not count
Or bid, through whom a passion stares
And feeds on what he cannot grasp:
Each penned or passing creature wears,
For him, an auric splendour, faint
But clear and there. His fingers clasp

A hand above him, trembling at
The power a solicitous father bends
To shield him from. But through the boy's
Passion – uncertain where it tends,
What it might mean – the man has caught
Something of brilliance, so that he toys

With likenesses, which grope and guess
At meaning: through such wintry light
As lingers in the frosted breath
Looping these mindless skulls, one might
(He fancies) look on blessedness.
What moves him though, beyond all myth,

Is what the bidders, were they to break
Silence, might judge beneath contempt –
The vacant, dumb docility
With which most other lives are stamped.
This powerlessness to choose or speak
So fleshes out the verb *to be*

That children innocent of pain
Take it for glory: which, absurd
To traders who provide for them,
Seems emblem of a fate endured
To those who dream of angels on
The darkened hills of Bethlehem.

Christmas Eve, 1983

Birdsong and Polyphony

The birds in this illuminated manuscript –
Wood-dove and song-thrush, chaffinch and goldfinch –
Are radiant marginalia that gloss
The notion of music, the notation of music.

We take it that their natural artifice
Would drench creation in polyphony;
They perch at the white borders of the page,
The score behind them, held back from flight.

The Infinite Variety

1. THE MUSEUM OF NATURAL HISTORY, SANTA BARBARA

for Edgar Bowers

All the birds of the region in one room,
Condor to humming-bird! Only a glance takes in
Pelican, golden eagle, blue-jay, wren...
Two hundred maybe, stuffed, posed, poised for flight.
What need (you say) has nature for so many
Exquisite variations? She selects
Each kind, are we to think, by fine distinction –
In the whole country, say, some forty species
Of warbler, each a different intersection
Of colour, music, mass, texture and form?
Or was it some such randomness as jars
Through the San Andreas Fault, which will in time
Shatter this state of high prosperity
To nameless this and that: did some such flaw
Cause these named rifts, that branch in plenitude?

2. MINERALS FROM THE COLLECTION OF JOHN RUSKIN

The boy geologist who clove the rocks
Here on display grew up to be the great
Philosopher of colour into form
And, in the products of just workmanship,
Discerned the paradigm of the just state.

It was the Lord's design he made apparent –
These bands and blocks of azure, umber, gilt,
Set in their flexing contours, solid flow
That had composed itself in its own frame:
Red garnet neighbouring mica, silver white;
A slice of agate like an inland sea...

In manhood, similarly, his eye judged how
Good stone splits fairly at the mason's touch;
How painters stay their colour, shape the run
And blotch of it to images of truth.
He taught that these, and others like them, might
– Workers with hand or mind – be driven less
By harsh need or harsh fate than by the call
Imagination hears to make new worlds:
Which honour in epitome this world,
Ruled by its fluid and elusive forms.

If chance be providential, the taught eyes
Of those who paint or carve so should instruct us
In justice and original design.

3. MY FATHER'S COLLECTION OF INDIAN BUTTERFLIES AND MOTHS

for Val

I have no names for them, foreign to me,
Although my father named and numbered each.
Nor, now they are gone, can I recall
One individual insect – neither shape
Nor colour nor composition. So I brood
On formless memories of moths so big
They looked like two splayed hands linked at the thumbs,
And butterflies arranged by deviation
From an unstated norm of their design:
You could imagine them – they were so vibrant –
Cut from some miniature of Shah Jahan's.

I was three when my father died; my mother
Outlived him forty years. When she died too,
My sister and I brought down the insect boxes –
Perhaps in expectation that that vision
Of plenitude, long stowed, awaited us.
I could not breathe to think of them. We opened
To nothing but a hint of dust, and pins
Staked upright, row on row, like monuments
To that which he had left us, though it felt
As if what he had left us had not been.

The Thirst

A kingfisher darting the green scum on a pool
Leaves it unbroken. Out of and over long grass
An erratic career, and a hare has become distance.

These things should be enough. But the old Adam
In me calls for their naming, seeing in them
Not at all more than their being there, but more
Than that they are. The one lust we can never
Wholly contain. The one unquenchable thirst.

The body barely withdrawn from the spring of delight,
And a full silence. Unbroached it cannot be.

To Robert Wells

on his translation of The Georgics

This is your poem of fields and flocks and trees
(As it was Virgil's) for the words are yours,
If words are of a poet, which are ours
And not ours either but the names of things.

A Catalogue of Flowers

WILD FLOWERS

Ragwort and mallow, toadflax and willow herb
Trick out the wasteground patchwork that I thread
To no end, not for delight, but with a passion
Such as they feel who are obsessed with death –

Though this is not death. I linger here
Where rot assumes these terrace-house cadavers,
And brick-rubble, riven paving-slabs, puddled ruts
Are cordoned off by bindweed tapestries

On looms of fence-wire. One might think neglect
Cultivates that for which it has made way –
The minor glories idleness in passing
Names: 'wallflower', 'dogrose', maybe 'traveller's joy'.

BINDWEED SONG

I am convolvulus.
I prosper where your ways are undermined
By war or social lapse. So call me weed:
Bindweed that comes uncalled for, weeds that bind.

Where eyesores are I flourish –
Where mildew, rat and spider occupy
Your seat and artefact. They are the world,
You the ephemerids, and what am I

Who have wound a way back in?
– Who mesh and drape (until they all cohere)
Hedge, pathway and door-frame. See, passer-by,
How beauty decks the substance of your fear.

AN AUTUMN VISION

In dreams, in bombed-out houses,
Where childhood used to play,
Among brambles and briar roses
And grass running to seed I pick my way,

Until I reach a clearing
Of strafed and harrowed ground
Where tombs founder, smoke blackened,
Corroded angels mourning, and no sound.

Finding the grave – a broadsword
Laid on memorial loam
As the tomb cross – and leaning forward
To gouge the sooty lichen from a name,

I glimpse beyond in the greenwood
Some purple artifice
(A helmet plume?) flourishing over
The drawn, despairing, honourable face

Of one whose quest advances
Down broken paths that tend
Towards a past locked in battle
With wrong he knows no future can amend.

POST-WAR CHILDHOODS

for Takeshi Kusafuka

*If there were no affliction in this world we might
think we were in paradise.*

Simone Weil, *Gravity and Grace*

You, born in Tokyo
In nineteen forty-four,
Knew the simplicity
Occasioned by a war.
In London it was so
Even in victory –
In defeat, how much more.

Knew it I say – and yet,
Born to it, you and I,
How could we in truth have known?
It was the world. You try
To make articulate,
In language not your own,
What it was like and why.

Nature returned (you say)
To downtown Tokyo –
In your voice, some irony
Defending your need to go
That far: what other way
Of like economy
Is there of saying so?

Your images declare
The substance of the phrase:
Bomb craters, urban grass,
A slowworm flexing the gaze
Of the boy crouching there;
Moths, splayed on the glass,
Like hands lifted in praise.

A future might have drawn
On what such things could tell.
You heard, even as you woke,
Accustomed birdsong fill
The unpolluted dawn,
Heard a toad bloat and croak
In some abandoned well.

They call it desolation,
The bare but fertile plot
You have been speaking of.
You grew there, who have taught
Me much of the relation
Affliction bears to love
In Simone Weil's scoured thought.

I, too, have images.
A photograph: St Paul's,
The dome a helmeted head
Uplifted, as terror falls.
The place I knew, not this
But a city back from the dead,
Grew fireweed within walls.

I played over dead bombs
In suburban villas, a wrecked
Street of them where, run wild,
Fat rhododendrons cracked
The floors of derelict rooms:
It seemed to a small child
An Eden of neglect.

If we two share a desire,
It is not that either place,
Still less the time, should return.
If gravity and grace
Survive a world on fire
Fixed in the mind, they burn
For things to be in peace.

CONSERVANCY
    for Heather Glen

*It was the treatment of the banks by the Thames Conservancy
Board, which regularly cut down all the flowers and cleared
the stream of its pleasant flowering reeds and rushes, which
so enraged Morris.*

                    Philip Henderson, *William Morris*

'These were the buds that tipped desire
And shaped what might be from what is.
Now summer grants the river's edge
This wealth of colour: bullrushes,

Long purples, a strong yellow flower
That's close and buttony, horse mint,
Mouse ear, belated meadow-sweet,
And dark blue mug-wort – not a hint

Of luxury in the excess
That freshens in the passing gust,
Or anarchy in the design
Of that which grows where grow it must.

Yet now the Thames Conservancy,
Subversive of this perfect state,
Instructs the servile ministers
Of order to annihilate

These frail entanglements, this fine
Community of loveliness,
Where natural harmony, though not
Traceable, governs nonetheless.

I loose my anger, then withdraw
To dream the paradise within:
Rich banks of colour that declare
Proudly a humble origin

Without – I weave them from the dark
And so, approximately, chart
The paradise we share, whose stream
Rises and rises in the heart.'

ALKANET

for Di

I'd seen it before but had not heard it named:
The leaves like nettles, a blue flower that peers
Above dustbins and detritus. Called alkanet,
It's a kind of wild borage, the book says.

A year, more or less, since we moved in.
That long June evening, you having gone back
To the old house, I stayed on sanding the floor
Until I could no longer see to work,

Then for the first time left by the back way.
Anxiety dulled by labour, conscious alone
Of sweat and dust and my limbs' weight, I felt
The quiet that is exhaustion coming on

And in the alley, among dark shapes of leaf –
Palpable shadows that I waded through,
My hands tingling – saw tiny flowers that retained
The sky's late intensity of blue.

When I got home I told you of the flowers
And of the light I'd seen them in. Since then
I know you have often thought of them as mine,
Not seeing that I cared for them as yours.

TO PAINT A SALT MARSH

Samphire and mare's tail and the salt marsh.

Nothing appears to have movement here
but the birds – it is where the white tern
pivots his swift course and on the tideline
dunlin and sandpiper dibble.
                              Otherwise,
at low tide, it's as if the brown sea
clogged in the mudflats. A spar,
tall and near the vertical, splits the view.

And on the horizon a grass-thatched sand-dune
looms like a northern fell. It
lays on the water's stillness precisely
its own stillness.

Work

For Donald Davie
sculptor in verse

1

Adam,
in the sweat of his brow,
ate bread.

Eve, in pain,
laboured
to bear fruit.

She spun, she wove...
Adam carved:

not that the stones
be made bread,
but rather

that (stone worked
and habitation
hewn from it)

bread be eaten,
fruit borne.

2

At the point of the chisel
what was
a block of stone
a corbel, a capital
becomes
pierced with darkness
a leafy glade
               of the forest
brought indoors

And beneath it, cut
from the general view
for God
for the swineherd your brother,
(where an acorn-cup empty
tells of the forest floor)
two pigs
　　　　　　two snouts rather
rooting among leaves

3
A mullion —
cleft and branching, then
in the marble
cut leafage, un-
furling
　　　　clear of it

Such needless beauty
the Protestant work ethic
has no time for

Though it was hand
and labour first
bowed the mason
to the task

Which issues in this praise
of the maker of leaves and stone

The Law of the House

A house of good stone
cut fair and square,
Justice the governor –

spotless, abstract,
a goddess held in common
by all people. And all

particulars too, by virtue
of being, acknowledge
her true sway. As economy

is house law, it follows
that builders should dispose
with precision – that is,

lapidary justice.
It is a scene in fresco –
equable rule

there, figured
by impartial light
and clear space. But if

the contrasted masses
move, clash, if the ground quake
and dislodge stone,

if storm
set person against
person or against thing,

what syntax in confusion
can piece together
the logic of her dark will?

At the Grave of Ezra Pound

S. Michele, Venice

1

here lies a man
of words, who in time
came to doubt their meanings

who therefore confines
himself to two words
only here

EZRA POVND

minimal
the injury done
to the white stone

none
to the earth
it rests upon

2

The spoils of a corsair –
who ranged the Mediterranean
and brought home
porphyry, alabaster, lapis lazuli
and every hue and current of veined marble.

In the bayleaves' shade
dumb now
and within earshot
of the stilled Adriatic
deaf, rests
under white marble
la spoglia, the remains.

At the Grave of William Morris

Kelmscott Churchyard

1

where you lie
        northman
your grey gable
rugg'd with lichen

roof raised above
        no walls,
soul's shelter
from the sky's bluster,

and there underneath it
        rests
that restless body
rootless among roots

2

Through the mouth and nostrils
sprouts greenery

or rime glitters
in the great beard

Desire

like ivy on a gravestone
binds him to this one place

like grass threading
the bluebells and the cowslips
braids him into it –

this holy place,
made holier by
his love of it

by his love

Fonte Branda in Siena

Ruskin, *Praeterita* III, iv, §86
Dante, *Inferno* xxx, 49-90

Fonte Branda, wrote Ruskin, *I last saw*
under the same arches where Dante saw it.
He drank of it then
                  and every time the near
pentameters of his prose recur to me,
I too see the place again:

the *loggia* of red brick, in white stone
the jutting bestial heads
                and within,
shade and the still pool.

Whenever the Englishman went there he would find
rage at injustice,
true words that pinion falsehood and cupidity,
bitterness in the sweet spring, the hiss
of white hot metal plunged in the cool water
as he drank.
             I think of that sad face,
the charred brain behind it, the word-flow.
And in my thought, as if toward the calm
of memory, he stoops to drink.
And every time he stoops the Florentine
in his pink coat, not crowned with laurel yet,
moves into range
                much as another's words
return to the quiet mind.

They do not see me there. But the place names
hold them in view – *Siena, Fonte Branda* –
by brimming water, on the point of speech.

A Plaque

Pensione Calcina, Venice

In this house lived   in 1877

JOHN RUSKIN

High-priest of art
in the stones of Venice   in her St Mark's
in almost every monument in Italy
he sought   at one and the same time
the craftsman's soul and the soul of the craftsman's people.

Every block of marble bronze-casting and canvas
every thing proclaimed aloud to this man's senses
that beauty is religion
if human virtue sustain it
and a reverent people acknowledge it.

The Commune of Venice   in recognition
XXVI January MDCCC

From the Italian

To a Poet from Eastern Europe, 1988

Strong drink –
on the bare table a neat vodka,
Innocently transparent as pure water,
Shimmers before you, with your fence of bone
(Stake shoulders, propping arms) set up around it,
As if, out there alone,
The spirit needed body to defend it.

From where I stand, though, I can count the cost
(The soured breath, sickly flush and hollow chest)
You pay, at 45, for what you savour.
It fortifies, calms the stomach, and yet still
         – Alas! greybeard cadaver –
Consumes the body as pure spirit will.

Consider, as you waste, how we are stewards
Of our bodies, yes, yet strangely how you thrive
On the sick body politic your words
Bite into as you're bitten: how your thirst
         For truth keeps you alive,
Writhing in anger, choking on disgust.

To Haydn and Mozart

You were both endowed with flair and with, no doubt,
What is called genius; but I think of you
Bent over your claviers, two men at work,
Fending off discord with your fingertips.
At work you could stay unmoved by what you knew
Of exploitation or of penury,
Uncomprehending ignorance and pride,
Loss, disappointment, pain. You turned from these
To forms your labour could not warp, because
You heard in them the possibility
Of grace, which echoes order in the mind.

The Kitchen Table

in memory of my Mother

Making a home was
what you could do
best; and cookery

(the ritual at
the heart of it) you had
a kind of genius for.

So what I first
recall, thinking of you,
is a creamy table-top,

the grain etched
crude and deep, the legs
stained black, and you

at work, with rolling-pin
or chopping-board or
bowl; then, later,

presiding over
guests or children at each
day's informal feast.

Your homeliness
displaced now, what survives
for me of it

is this: which
now becomes a model
of true art:

bare boards scrubbed clean,
black, white,
good work as grace, such

purity of heart.

Charon's Bark

to my Mother

1

It's the being left behind
I can't believe:
me stranded on this shore
and glimpsing you,
too far out, too baffled by the crowd
of they might be twittering shoppers,
to notice that I stay.

I recognise you by
a look of panic, so faint
who else in the world would notice it,
as you stare back at the shore,
your set eyes blind to the same look
in these that reach out after you.

2

On nights like this,
when with snow piled deep it is
too cold to snow any more
in the bitter wind,
I can't get the thought of you out of my mind.

What I keep thinking of
is waking too early on a bright morning,
and running to your bed, and jumping in.

On nights like this,
I can't keep the tears back
at the thought of you –
out there in the dark, the snow your coverlet,
unwakably asleep.

Two Journals

I keep two journals. In the first one there's
A record of dreams, fantasies and fears
That edge me toward that commonplace, the Brink:
My evidence, that is, for beak or shrink.

On odd days in the second – now more odd,
Alas, than ordinary – I brood on God,
The distant prospect of his love, and bend
Aesthetics and poetics to that end.

Sadly I can't conflate them in one text.
There I am crazed, erratic, oversexed,
Here pure, serene and earnest in my quest;
An angel here, there a tormented beast!

So when I write in one, I overlook
Evidence set down in the other book.
So they, between the two of them, divide
The single mind where single truths reside.

The Temple of Aphrodite

1

I woke to nobody. Desire. Intent.
And her to follow as embodiment.

2

Twilight. The streets invite me. They run down
Towards the harbour. In the heart of town

Some common land where road and quayside merge.
A kestrel weighs above. On a grass verge

A rabbit, tempted out, soon bobs away.
I drift back to the shopfronts. Now the day

Is switched off, starker lights illumine whores
Who, between open street and shuttered doors,

Poise, whispering incitements. Manliness,
Withdrawn and shy, rises to the caress

Of smooth obscenity, that heady charm,
Which leads me, not to pleasure nor to harm,

But down an inward subway, a deep maze
Of infinitely bifurcating ways.

3

I meet you in a room too dark for shame
And call you Love, who have no other name.

4

Naked, it feels as if some filmy dress
Still clung invisibly to her bare flesh.

It is like language clothed in irony:
Her body – smooth, particular and free –

Is offered in the name of love, might seem
The incarnation of a general dream;

Yet, though I tremble at her skilled caress,
I know I am not the object of address.

5

What you find – making love, with no love meant –
Is contact without cóntent; without contént.

6

An hour before my train. Leaving the car,
I cross the station to a burger bar

That looks out on the street. I sit and read –
Drink tea, drink good strong prose, and do not heed

The garish colours round me or outside
The urgent traffic at its fullest tide.

Combatively my book affirms the good
Of this world's substance – always understood,

First, that the mind which loves the world is more
Than what it loves; and then (in a sense the core

Of such love) that if earthly powers deny
Our love its freedom, we are free to die.

O but it's dark already. Across the way
She stands, under a streetlamp, on display,

A handsome woman, black, in red high heels;
A string vest of the self-same red reveals,

More than it clothes, her breasts' full luxury,
And skin-tight silver ski-pants generously

Outline her other curves, from hip to calf.
I rise, contemplative, then stand and laugh

In the doorway. Words gone, the train can go.
What else in the wide world could move me so?

Amores

I call this latest book Adversity.
Though it is mine, it is obscure to me.
Some passages of love, though, seem more clear
In a dark context, and I gloss them here.

*

It was not quite the last time. Yet, that day,
Orgasm shook my body with a cry
That echoed through me like a long goodbye.
We parted; then you wept, and turned away.

*

We first met maybe seven years ago
But barely more than chatted before this.
Three afternoons of love, and you must go.
I miss you, scarcely knowing whom I miss.

*

Those brieze-block walls: bare in my memory
The room is – basin, bed, one lamp, one chair.
Yet, entering it, I found you also bare,
And lay down in the lap of luxury.

*

Strange that of all things I recall this fact:
Neither the surge of passion nor the act,
But falling asleep like a child no terrors shake,
Who can, because the woman stays awake.

*

Despising though desiring you, I let
Our next date pass, deciding to forget.
I'd known you, say, five hours in fewer days;
Twenty years later, how you touched me stays.

*

I see a broken city in your head
(Beautiful lady) ravaged by cross-fire.
But here, against that backdrop, you are led
By civil urgencies of sweet desire.

*

You speak of hope and liberty, new love.
Why must I speak of loyalty and despair?
Freedom is our two bodies as they move
And hopelessness the passion we must share.

*

I thought myself unscathed, so did not yield,
But ran till, looking back from a safe height,
I saw wrenched bodies on a battlefield
That once had seemed a garden of delight.

*

Dear child, dear lady, bless you where you sleep
Alone, who should be sleeping here with me.
My one desire's that your desire should keep
On beating at the gates of reverie.

Re-reading my Poem 'Saxon Buckle'

My amulet against the shocks of time!
I made it twenty years ago and still
Despair and terror, snared in the taut rhyme,
Are held by that old exercise of skill.

I trawled for meaning in the world out there
From then till now. The changing world's changed me.
And still, through emptiness, my words declare:
'Meaning is ours: in this space you are free.'

Transference

for Graham Davies

A moving tableau, so to speak.
On the same couch, week after week,
Talking of absence, I can see
Its likeness bearing down on me:
The ceiling blankness. But if I
Let my glance fall to where the sky
Through the broad window hangs behind
The web of garden life, I find
Love I'd thought dead diffused among
Bright songbirds; they with inhuman song
And vivid colour, as they feed
At the bird-table, hit my need
For harmony. And then your voice
Behind me, beyond reach of choice,
Speaks out of darkness and dismay.
De profundis, Domine.

The Dream

Under those heads, an argument of coils,
Protean, polymorphous, serpentine.
Hot breath, bared teeth: the questioning is mine,
The questions not. I strike. A neck recoils,

Gives way before my answer. Thus I hack
Into the bloated flesh of it: thus, thus.
Winged helmet, carven shield: the fabulous
Purity, grace and swiftness of attack!

And still the heads. Day breaks. And no respite.
The questions, now I flag, metamorphose,
The asker changes, then the monster goes,

And still the coils are there, a wraith in light.
I rise, I dress for work; blunt sword, cracked shield.
No more than whisper and the worm's revealed.

In the Greenwood

*In August 1987, a 27 year-old gun-collector named
Michael Ryan shot a young woman dead in Savernake
Forest. There was no obvious motive. That same day he killed
fifteen other people, including his mother, in the nearby
town of Hungerford. He ended by committing suicide.*

When Michael Ryan in that forest glade
(Armed and flak-jacketed, his camouflage
Not disentangled quite from leafy shade)
Let out the first spurt of his huge discharge,

He invoked Emptiness: in these dull days
Prince of this land and Regent (for the King
Must brood in exile on our ancient ways
And the green woods of their meandering).

Now, as the echoes die, I hear a man
My countrymen once dreamt of wind his horn –
A note of warning from a vanished wood;

He, gentle yet pugnacious, jovial
And stubbornly enduring, gave up all
His right and fortune to the common good.

1988

The Garden

Efface complexity, forget the bond
Of old affection, trust, ennui...For love,
This room's the world: which all the world beyond,
Although enriched by it, knows nothing of.

Your body is the garden at its heart:
Sweetness and pungency; earth in this place
Is damp, springy with moss, and when I part
The leaves up there, fruit dangles in my face.

Such innocence! But, now you stretch and yawn
And rise, you turn away from me toward
The somewhere-else that is to be endured.
The world is all before us. We shall meet
A messenger with news of our deceit
Where pale flowers shred and tangle on the thorn.

Oasis

The terms of the analogy are strained –
And that is as it should be, for the world
Is nothing but the world and things are called
By names they cannot answer to. Constrained
By what I am to name things, when I see
How beauty proper to a watered place
Extends beyond it to this wilderness
I call this paradise, which it can't be.

And it is paradise I think of too
When your cool body's fluency and grace
Come near, and nearer, in this desert place
As if the Lord were beckoning through you –
    Though God is darkest when his creatures bless
    And paradise is of the wilderness.

The Earth Rising

The men who first set foot on the bleached waste
That is the moon saw rising near in space
A planetary oasis that surpassed
The homesick longings of their voyaging race:

Emerald and ultramarine through a white haze
Like a torn veil – as if no sand or dust
Or stain of spilt blood or invading rust
Corrupted it with reds, browns, yellows, greys.

So visionaries have seen it: to design
Transparent, luminous and, as if new-made,
Cut from surrounding darkness. Praise the Lord,
For *Heaven and earth* (the psalmist sang) *are thine;*
The foundation of the round world thou hast laid,
And all that therein is. And plague and sword.

New Poems

To Thom Gunn, on his 60th Birthday

You won't recall them now – 'The Burial Mound',
'Valhalla', 'The Dead Warrior' – poems which sound
Too much like half-cooked, over-seasoned stews
Of tough ingredients culled from Gunn and Hughes
('Thistles', 'The Byrnies', 'The Warriors of the North',
'The Wound'). Hard man, you read my pourings-forth,
Gauche as they were, with such strict tolerance,
Such courtesy, you never looked askance
At what, derived from you, partook of truth
Though twisted through the fantasies of youth;
You taught me form, reminding me of sense
When rhetoric or modish violence
Deformed a phrase or rhythm; you deferred
To nothing but economy of word.

But that was not the start of it. I had
At seventeen – such a discerning lad! –
Looked for your poems in the library
And found *The Sense of Movement* by Gunn, T.
I read it with mixed feelings, much impressed
By rigour – by the epithets that dressed
Your heroes for attack, more than by what
I now admire as rigour in the thought –
Yet doubting if such toughness was OK
For arty liberals of that latter day.
Then *My Sad Captains* showed me how the wise
Must reason toughly, since they recognise
Unreason in the will, desire and sleep,
And know the limits of the calm they keep.

Soon afterwards we met. I was nineteen
And still a stranger to the poetry scene.
You were in London in the happy year
Of 'Talbot Road', and over pints of beer
Two or three nights we talked of poetry –
Image and metre, gossip and history.
I boasted somewhat, mainly listening though.
Later I realised you'd begun to go
Down new paths to new lines and loyalties:

Looser, though still demanding, more at ease
With what you are and how you have your say.
Famous and thirty-five, your year away
From home and love gave you a second start,
Your learning still unfinished, like your art.

Happy the man of sixty who still sees
Himself as learning! Streetwise Socrates,
You who know nothing and have taught so much,
Twenty-four years now you have kept in touch
Through intermittent letters (meetings rare)
And written off my debts as goods we share.
I tried to imitate your 'mighty line',
Poetic hero, might have made it mine,
Hoping thereby to teach myself a role,
Like you to manufacture my own soul...
Until your new lines, tentative, explored
Like hands in darkness, groping word by word
To touch on things that lie beyond the reach
Of words, though not to wrench them into speech.

Now as our century, blasé with despair,
Broaches its last decade, the troubled air
Trembles with rumour of disastrous ends.
Where you live, with your family of friends,
A plague rules, and it leaves you little choice
But to make death your text, when to rejoice
In ripeness might have suited your old age.
Well, it *is* ripe (since only years assuage
Our grief) to live like you, without regret;
For which I honour you, still in your debt,
And being in part by earlier works consoled:
Those gorgeous metamorphoses, as gold
As California your side of the range,
The sand beyond it undisturbed by change.

1989

104

Letter to J.A. Cuddon*

on his retirement
from schoolteaching

Dear Charles,
                 I've had you on my mind this year.
A recent shift into the festive gear
Has meant I've seen much more of you, and then
I've found myself reading your books again:
One novel, which you say is not your best
But which has passages – for me the test –
That fixed me to my chair, freezing my arms;
Your *Dictionary of Literary Terms*
(Revised), as good a book for the bedside
As many a novel is; and last, your Guide
To a Jugoslavia scarred with memories
Even in relatively sunlit days.
You raise the question on your opening pages:
How the South Slavs have wrought, across the ages,
Such violence on each other and yet face
Strangers with courtesy, tolerance and grace...
Reading I felt at once that the real world
Was there, in those quiet words – and that recalled
School and the way it seemed you never thought
That you were teaching: which is how you taught.
And yes, of course, the other reason why
You've occupied my thoughts is, this July,
You leave the school where – dare I let folk know? –
You taught me more than thirty years ago.

    The model classroom teacher you were not.
If you'd learnt teaching methods, you forgot
To make much use of them: of talk and chalk,
Your preference was plainly for the talk.
Such talk it was! You would, with text in hand,
In gruffly stylish sentences expand

---

* J.A. Cuddon, known to his friends as Charles, is a writer, traveller and schoolmaster. His publications include five novels, two dictionaries and two travel books: *The Owl's Watchsong: A Study of Istanbul* (1960) and *The Companion Guide to Jugoslavia* (1968).

On what we had to read, at times digress,
Not so much analyse. So you'd address –
In Hopkins, say – morphologies of line,
The erotic love that figures the divine,
Grey falcons stooping, the Ignatian rule,
Forms literary and biological –
All of the things, in short, I wished to know
Or thought I should, once you had sketched them so.

You did your job, then, also coached a team
(Rugby or cricket), but did not ever seem
Quite *of* the school. Our *Führer* of a Head
(You wryly told me) used to cut you dead
In the corridor – or else you'd be required
At once to see your barber. I *admired*
What must have niggled him: your tattered gown,
The perpetual cigarette, and the slight frown
(Not without humour) that told less of care
Than of the mental life you lived elsewhere –
The books and journeys out beyond the gate
At the drive's end. Indeed, you turned up late
Each autumn term – though just in time to teach –
Tanned like a bather on a southern beach,
Having come (went the rumour) straight to school
From the last sleeper out of Istanbul.

I would not say that you were dissident –
Just that, maybe, a habit of dissent
Showed in your conduct. For you spared the rod
And if, to our surprise, you talked of God,
Yours was a Roman cosmopolitan,
Who made the Chaplain's by comparison
Seem a provincial...Be that as it may,
For me these sparks ignited in a play:
How well do you remember *The Dumb Waiter*?
Some consternation in the *alma mater*
Was caused by your production of it: *hard*
It seemed in '62, too *avant-garde*
And Beckettishly weird. What did it *mean*?
Was there perhaps a god in that machine?
Did he exact day-labour, light denied?
Were blasphemies like Pinter's justified

By *deeper meanings*? Such fatuity
Seemed to your actors – just Steve Gooch and me –
Appalling, though no doubt outraged surprise
Fed our young vanities. You, worldly wise,
Grunted ironically – you would, of course –
And on the last night led us, after hours,
Up to the staff room where your *bonhomie*
Invited us to share a fine Chablis.
This disinclined us to take much to heart
Those slight distresses which the life of art
Inflicts on its adherents: it's a test
That poet, novelist and dramatist
Must pass before they ripen. Don't complain
Of losses, wordsmith; drink deep when you gain.

   A wordsmith, Charles. That strikes me as a fair
Description of you, yet I'm well aware
That earlier I spoke of gruffness too.
I mean a reticence I find in you –
Not unbecoming in a soldier's son –
Which edges all your words. I think of one
Lesson when you contrasted styles of verse.
The note of conversation, plain and terse,
Was what you favoured. The luxuriant –
In music as in sensuous ornament –
You admired too, for richness and for skill,
But had your reservations. I can still
Hear you chastise as *facile* and as *glib*
The sort of bard who runs off at the nib.
New to me at that age, the two words stuck
As you had used them, emblems of my luck
In being taught by one whose words were weighed
Like ingots of great price; and this has made
You present in those words whenever, since,
I've found them used precisely in that sense.
That, I suppose, is what it is to teach –
Not only how to use words but that speech
Is difficult. We use words to mean things,
And something more than that which soothes and sings
Informs good poems – they are answerable
To fact, which is resistant to the will.
I learnt from you to value stubbornness

And to judge best those works that bear the impress
Of silence in their margins. Can't you see
How I must fight to ward off fluency? –
For instance in this letter here, which I've
Composed in celebration. Believe me,

Clive

1993

Anthem

Suppose him to be a person
whose whole faith is in words,
yet at weekday evensong
           a devout attender,

loving the stained demise
of daylight, as it transfigures
the Gothic walls' pale stone
           with watercolour

and the silhouetted wings
spread in the rafters, resounding
to the voices of boys, their poly-
           phonic ascent.

Then consider him to have heard
an anthem one day, the text
being several lines perhaps
           of his own writing

set to such notes as thwart
the sadness at day's end
with glory (as it were)
           oh *in excelsis*

by a friend to whom a composed
harmony is for the soul
the one lodging, brief but secure,
           on its brief journey.

Psalm

Here the waters converge and in their fork
       we sit on the ground and weep.
          So this is exile.

Their currents flow by me. Why should they heed
       a man in love with the past
          of his own country,

lost to him now, elsewhere? Our home river,
       gone underground, flows counter.
          And when our masters –

half in mockery, yet half curious
       to hear such foreign lore –
          call for an old song,

I hang my harp high on a willow bough
       leaning across the flood.
          Jerusalem,

let the hand that writes these verses wither and die
       if I forget you now
          in this ill time;

let my tongue stick in my throat if I sell short
       the source of all my words,
          fail to remember

where my joys began. In the mean time,
       Daughter of Babylon, you
          have humbled us:

you may publish us to the world, you may ignore us.
       But we have time. In time
          we will be revenged.

                          Psalm 137

The Manor House

'Ramshackle loveliness' was the phrase I wrote,
then cancelled and kept free for use elsewhere:
　　the whole feel of the place – as much
　　　　the countryside as his house –

is in that sense of unachieved perfection
and slight neglect that makes for beauty. It might be
　　the receding lip of a stone step
　　　　foot-worn to a wave,

or a tie-beam, the curved thew of a bough
black with pitch, or the way each block of stone
　　(crudely dressed, set on the soil
　　　　it was dug from time out of mind)

fits so closely yet roughly against stone.
I come outside and imagine him living there,
　　as the wind heaves and the loaded tree
　　　　lurches, towards the wall,

its freight of apples. In there, he draws or writes
and apple and grey stone are in his work
　　as leaves and feathers are, which seem
　　　　(ruffled in draught, the dust

blown from their pores) fresh from creation. What
is this I feel but love for the man he was
　　or must have been? The river willows
　　　　tense hard against the wind

as I drive by a rutted track for the M4:
it is only five miles off and yet (with the river,
　　clear as its source, flowing between)
　　　　might as well be a thousand.

Grace

When you spoke, after dinner,
of haymaking, of loading
the tractor at dusk and the
new fragrance of hay you breathed
in with delight (and so out

in your talk), first came to mind
my garden – the basil there
that stains my fingers with its
pungency, and washed linen
freshening on the line – and then,

on my way home, the prayer you
said before food, which again
now fills me with thanks, as if
savour or scent were the thought
no gift can be good without.

King Alfred's Book

A King made me. Alfred turned
Roman letters into English speech.
Now, as you read me,
Hear his voice and your mother-tongue
Telling the Roman's tale.

First you must hear: men once loved learning.
The word-hoards they harboured
Were great wealth to them, and solace –
Their books, jewelled and enamelled, richly gilded.
That time is gone.
You see their tracks but you cannot trace them.

Do not allow my unregarded leaves
To flutter in the wind and rain.
These lines of script are ways through the forest.
You, as you read me,
Keep the ways open.

Lindisfarne Sacked

The dragon prows. Dragons' tongues
    flare at the darkness:
       illumination.

House-Martin

   for M.L.

– like the heart's arrow,
    unerringly home
       to her nest in the ribbed vault.

The Pig Man

*Carmine Ferretti, aged 69, emerges on Saturday from
the pigsty near Atri, Central Italy, where he was kept
for sixty years by his family. Mr Ferretti, mute and
mentally retarded since childhood, had a disability
pension which the family shared.*

                                    Newspaper caption

The cameras flash and he lurches into light.
His feet clog in ordure. At sixty-nine,
He has long outlived the companions of his youth.

Look at him. The face is a scared face:
The brain behind it knows (that is to say)
No more than the world in which he finds himself.

His eyes seem to look out from the sides of his head.
They appear to focus on nothing. Head down,
He shambles forward as if led by the nose.

What is more human than a mind deranged?
Here is a mind that is innocent of thought.
What is man, that thou art mindful of him?

Thou hast made him a little lower than the angels
To crown him with glory and worship
And given him dominion over the beasts.

What is a man who knows no other warmth
Than the coarse and steaming flanks of a mother sow,
Our brother in the house of Brother Pig?

The policeman watching over him looks away.
He is sober and expressionless, on duty.
One can tell that he is mindful.

Kaspar Hauser

Who wanted to be a horseman
Who wanted to be what his father had been before him

Who had no father, who had no mother
Who could not ride
Who sprang fully-formed from nowhere

Who knew the floor of a stable
better than he knew the world or knew himself
Who could not tell who had fed him or sustained him

Who lacked speech
Who could not put into words
where he had come from or what was to be his end
Who could not describe the world
Who could not define it

On whom the sins of the fathers were visited
Who was innocent, who was fallen
Who now was to eat bread in the sweat of his face

Who was sub-normal, moronic, mentally disabled,
an inspired visionary, a wolf-boy, a child of God

Who had quickened in his mother's womb
to be flung wailing into the world
Who had fallen from nowhere
and found himself nowhere

Who could not say who had killed him
or why he had had to die

Translations

'I Hate and Love'

I hate and love. You may well ask why so.
I cannot say; the pain is what I know.

FROM THE ITALIAN OF ST FRANCIS OF ASSISI

Canticle of the Sun

O my good Lord, almighty and most high,
Thine are the praise, the honour and the glory
And thereto every blessing.
To thee alone are they due, thee they become,
And worthy is no man to give tongue to thy name.

Praise be to thee, my Lord, with all thou'st made,
And in especial Master Sun, our brother,
Who bringeth day, by whom thou givest light.
Comely he is and bright, of a great shining,
And in thy likeness doth he shape his meaning.

Praise be, my Lord, in Sister Moon and the stars:
In heaven thou mad'st them, costly and bright and fair.

Praise be, my Lord, in Brother Wind and the air
In cloudy and clear sky and in all weathers:
By him thou dost sustain life in thy creatures.

Praise be, my Lord, also in Sister Water,
Who serveth all, lowly and precious and pure.

Praise be, my Lord, also in Brother Fire,
Whereby thou dost illumine the night well,
And he is handsome and jocund, strong and hale.

Praise be, my Lord, in our sister, Mother Earth,
Who nurtureth and governeth us all.
So many kinds of fruit she bringeth forth
With grass and with bright flowers.

Praise be, my Lord, in them who for thy love
Forgive and bear much pain and tribulation.
Blest who bear such in peace, most high,
For by thy hand shall they be crowned in heaven.

Praise be, my Lord, in Sister Death.
None living can escape her.
Woe to all them that die in mortal sin.
Blest whom she findeth in thy holy will —
The second death shall not harm them.

Give thanks to my Lord, bless him, sing his praise,
And serve him humbly all your days.

FROM THE ITALIAN OF DANTE

Sestina

I have come now to the long arc of shadow
And the short day, alas, and where the hills
Whiten, the colour gone from the old grass;
Yet my desire is constant in its green,
It has so taken root in the hard stone
That speaks and hears as if it were a woman.

Similarly this miracle of woman
Stays frozen like the deep snow left in shadow:
For she is no more moved than is a stone
By the sweet season – that which warms the hills
Turning the whiteness of them into green
And decking them in wild flowers, herbs and grass.

When her hair is garlanded with woven grass,
She draws the mind away from other women:
She braids the rippling yellow with the green
So beautifully, Love lingers in their shadow –
Love, who confines me here between low hills
More stringently than mortar binding stone.

Her beauty holds more power than precious stones
And nothing remedies – not herb or grass –
The hurt she gives: so over plain and hill
I have fled, my one need to escape that woman,
But from her eyes' clear light have found no shadow
By mountain, wall or leafage dense with green.

There was a time I saw her dressed in green
In such a way she could have made a stone
Feel the great love I bear her very shadow;
I desired her, therefore, in a field of grass –
As much in love as ever any woman
Has been – and ringed about by lofty hills.

But rivers will flow back and climb their hills
Before this wood, which is both damp and green,
Will at my touch catch fire – as fair women
Are known to do; and I would sleep on stone
My whole life long and go feeding on grass
Only to see where her dress casts a shadow.

Whenever the hills cast their blackest shadow,
With lovely green she makes it, this young woman,
Vanish, as stones are hidden in the grass.

Dante to Love's Faithful

from the Vita Nuova

To every noble heart these words may move,
Each captive soul that looks into their theme,
I send – to learn how you interpret them –
This greeting in your Lord's name, which is Love.

The stars were shining clear, the starlit hour
Then on the point of passing was the third,
When suddenly Love in his own form appeared;
And to recall that form grips me with horror.

Happy Love seemed: I saw that in one hand
He clutched my heart, while she I love was laid
Across his arms, wrapped in a cloth and sleeping.

Then when he woke her, though she was afraid
He humbly fed the heart to her, which burned:
And as he went away, I saw him weeping.

FROM THE ITALIAN OF GUIDO CAVALCANTI

Cavalcanti's Reply*

All the nobility men may know on earth,
The joy, the good, it seems to me you saw;
That noble Lord was proving you, whose law
Commands the world of honourable worth.

For where he lives, harsh dreariness must die;
With reason he holds sway in the mind's keep.
No pain he causes when he comes in sleep
Gently to steal our hearts from where we lie.

* i.e. to the preceding poem, 'Dante to Love's Faithful'.

He stole your heart when she you worship was
Falling – he had perceived it – into death;
And fearing this, he gave it her to eat.

You saw him leave in sorrow then, because
Sweet sleep was on the point of ending with
The imperious advent of its opposite.

'I leave to the blind and deaf'

I leave to the blind and deaf
The soul with boundaries,
For I would feel all things
In all manner of ways.

I muse on earth and heaven
From heights of consciousness –
Innocent: for my eyes
Glimpse nothing I possess.

But I see, so intently –
Dispersed through what I see –
That in each thought I am,
At once, a different me.

And as those things are fragments
Of being in dispersion,
I split my soul up, each
Portion a different person.

And if I see my soul
With another view,
I ask, Is that a basis
For judgement that holds true?

Ah, just as for land and sea
And boundless sky. He errs
Who thinks himself his own.
Not mine, I am diverse.

Let me – if things are fragments
Of universal mind –
Be the pieces of myself,
Various, undefined.

If all I feel is other
And self apart from me,
How did the soul's end
Become identity?

Thus I conform to what
God's made from the first days;
God's way is different
And I am different ways.

Thus I ape God, who when
He made what is, withdrew
Infinity from it
And even oneness too.

'There was a rhythm in my sleep'

There was a rhythm in my sleep.
I have lost it – when I woke it went.
Why did I ever lead my life
Away from self-abandonment?

What was it, that which was not? I
Know that it lulled me sweetly then,
As though the very lulling sought
To make me who I am again.

Music there was which, when I woke
From dreaming it, broke off. The link,
Though, did not die: the theme goes on
In what impels me not to think.

from *The Keeper of Flocks*

by 'Alberto Caeiro'

IX

I am a keeper of flocks.
The flock is my thoughts
And my thoughts are all sensations.
I think with my eyes and with my ears
And with my hands and feet
And with my nose and mouth.

Thinking a flower is to see it and smell it
And eating a fruit is to taste its meaning.

That's why, on a hot day,
When I feel sad at so much delight,
And I stretch out on the grass
And close my warm eyes,
I feel my whole body stretched out in what's real,
I know the truth and I'm happy.

X

'Hey, keeper of flocks,
You, there at the roadside,
What does the wind tell you, passing by?'

'That it's the wind, and that it passes,
And that it's already passed before,
And that it'll pass again.
And what does it say to you?'

'A great deal more than that.
It speaks of so much more to me.
Of memories and desires
And of things that never were.'

'You've never heard the wind passing.
Wind is all that the wind speaks of.
What you heard it say was a lie,
And the lie is your own.'

'You who, Believing in your Christs and Marys'

by 'Ricardo Reis'

You who, believing in your Christs and Marys,
Trouble the limpid waters of my spring,
    And do so but to tell me
    That other kinds of water

In better times bathe meadows somewhere else –
Why speak to me of other realms if these
    Meadows and streams delight me
    And are of here and now?

The gods gave this reality, and gave it
This outwardness to make it real indeed.
    What are my dreams, if not
    Handiwork of the gods?

Leave me Reality, that is of the moment –
Also my tranquil and immediate gods
    Who do not live in Vagueness,
    But in fields, and in rivers.

Let life go by for me in pagan fashion
To the accompaniment of slender pipes
    Whereby the reedy banks
    Of streams acknowledge Pan.

Live in your dreams and leave me to the deathless
Altars whereon I make observances,
    Leave me the seen presence
    Of gods who are most near.

You who court vainly what excels this life,
Leave life to those with faith in something older
    Than Christ upon his cross
    And Mary weeping.

Comfort me, Ceres, lady of the fields,
Apollo, Venus, and archaic Uranus,
    And thunderbolts, compelling,
    Being from the hand of Jove.

FROM THE HUNGARIAN OF MIKLÓS RADNÓTI

A Mountain Garden

Summer has fallen asleep, it drones, and a grey veil
    Is drawn across the bright face of the day;
    A shadow vaults a bush, so my dog growls,
    His hackles bristling, and then runs away.

Shedding its petals one by one, a late flower stands
    Naked and half-alive; I hear the sound
    Of a withered apricot-bough crack overhead
    To sink of its own weight slowly to the ground.

O, and the garden too prepares for sleep, its fruit
    Proffered to the heavy season of the dead.
    It is getting dark. Late too, a golden bee
    Is flying a death-circle around my head.

And as for you, young man, what mode of death awaits you?
   Will a shot hum like a beetle toward your heart,
   Or a loud bomb rend the earth so that your body
   Falls limb from limb, your young flesh torn apart?

In sleep the garden breathes; I question it in vain;
   Though still unanswered I repeat it all.
   The noonday sun still flows in the ripe fruit
   Touched by the twilight chill of the dew fall.

[Istenhegy (a Buda mountain), 1936]

Forced March

A fool he is who, collapsed,   rises and walks again,
Ankles and knees moving   alone, like wandering pain,
Yet he, as if wings uplifted him,   sets out on his way,
And in vain the ditch calls him   back, who dare not stay.
And if asked why not, he might answer   – without leaving his path –
That his wife was awaiting him,   and a saner, more beautiful death.
Poor fool! He's out of his mind: now, for a long time,
Only scorched winds have whirled   over the houses at home,
The wall has been laid low,   the plum-tree is broken there,
The night of our native hearth   flutters, thick with fear.
O if only I could believe   that everything of worth
Were not just in my heart –   that I still had a home on earth;
If only I had! As before,   jam made fresh from the plum
Would cool on the old verandah,   in peace the bee would hum,
And an end-of-summer stillness   would bask in the drowsy garden,
Naked among the leaves   would sway the fruit-trees' burden,
And she would be waiting, blonde   against the russet hedgerow,
As the slow morning painted   slow shadow over shadow –
Could it perhaps still be?   The moon tonight's so round!
Don't leave me friend, shout at me: I'll get up off the ground!

[15 September 1944]

Postcard

No more than six or seven miles away
Haystacks and houses flare;
There, on the meadow's verges, peasants crouch,
Pipe-smoking, dumb with fear.
Here still, where the tiny shepherdess steps in,
Ripples on the lake spread;
A flock of ruffled sheep bend over it
And drink the clouds they tread.

[6 October 1944]

FROM THE POLISH OF CZESLAW MILOSZ

From a Notebook: Bon on Lake Geneva

Copper beeches, glistening poplars
And pine-trees steep above the October fog.
In the valley the lake steams. On the other side,
On mountain ridges, snow already lies.
What remains of life? Only this light,
Peculiar to sunny weather in this season,
Which makes you blink. People say: This *is* –
And there is neither skill nor talent
Able to reach beyond whatever *is*,
And unnecessary memories lose their strength.

A smell of cyder in barrels. The priest
Mixes lime with a spade outside the school.
By a path my son is running there. Boys carry
Sacks of chestnuts they have gathered from the slopes.
If I forget thee, O Jerusalem
(Saith the prophet), let my right hand wither.

An underground tremor shatters that which is:
Mountains crack, forests are rent asunder.
Touched by what was and by what will be,
What *is* crumbles into dust.
Violent, clean, the world is again in ferment,
And neither ambition nor memory will cease.

Autumn skies, who are the same in childhood,
The same in manhood and old age, I shall
Not look at you. And landscapes,
Who nourish the human heart with gentle warmth,
What poison is in you that lips are numb,
And arms folded across the chest, and eyes
Like a drowsy animal's. But whoever in what is
Finds peace, order and an eternal moment
Will vanish without trace. Do you agree then
To destroy what is and snatch the eternal moment
From flux – a gleam on the black river? I do.

FROM THE HUNGARIAN OF GYÖRGY PETRI

To Be Said Over and Over Again

I glance down at my shoe and – there's the lace!
This can't be gaol then, can it, in that case.

128

To Imre Nagy

You were impersonal, too, like the other leaders,
bespectacled, sober-suited; your voice lacked
sonority, for you didn't know quite what to say

on the spur of the moment to the gathered multitude. This urgency
was precisely the thing you found strange. I heard you,
old man in pince-nez, and was disappointed,
not yet to know

of the concrete yard where most likely the prosecutor
rattled off the sentence, or
of the rope's rough bruising, the ultimate shame.

Who can say what you might have said
from that balcony? Butchered opportunities
never return. Neither prison nor death
can resharpen the cutting edge of the moment

once it's been chipped. What we can do, though, is remember
the hurt, reluctant, hesitant man
who nonetheless soaked up
anger, delusion
and a whole nation's blind hope,

when the town woke to gunfire
that blew it apart.

Daydreams

Into destruction I would bring
an order whole and classical.
Hope for the good? Out of the question.
Let me die invisible.

Sors bona nihil aliud. To
whoever digs my bones I send
a message: which is, Look how all
God's picture-images must end.

And no there cannot be a heaven,
or else there oughtn't to be one
for, if there were, this plague of love
would still (come what may) go on.

Nor do I want the obverse – hell –
though of that I've had, will have, my bit
(planks beneath the chainsaw wail).

For anything unready, yet
ready too, I lie in the sun:
let the redeeming nowhere come.

FROM THE BULGARIAN OF LYUBOMIR NIKOLOV

Scaling Carp

Slowly the knife's grown over with blood and scales.
I grasp it tight, I flay
and try not to meet the eyes
of these mute creatures.
I flay just as I'd shave
pig's skin – against the bristle.
I take off the golden armour
to see their shining bodies underneath –
sleek, soft, naked.
On my shirt and trousers, scales.
They fly about me like wet chaff,
coating my face and shoes.
And I remember an old icon:

the dry gully, the two butterflies,
the dragon
pinned to the ground by St George's lance,
the small dog with the pink tongue
licking the dark clots.
Beside me, a bowl of flour –
I dredge the fish in it.
Through their white shirts
break blue ribs of blood.
It's noon.

And the oil's already boiling.

FROM THE GERMAN OF RAINER MARIA RILKE

Archaic Torso of Apollo .

Not to be known, the inconceivable
Head that the eyes ripened in. Yet the torso
Is like a branching gas-lamp, glowing still,
In which his gaze, no more than turned down low,

Burns on, gleams. Else it could not dazzle so,
The curved swell of the chest; nor could there be
In the slight twist of the loins a smile that goes
Toward the fulcrum that was potency.

Else the stone would not stand, disfigured, lopped,
Beneath the shoulders' lucid plunge and rush
And would not glisten like a wild beast's pelt;

And would not from its proper contours thus
Break like a star: for there is nowhere safe
From being seen here. You must change your life.

'Say, poet, what it is you do'

Say, poet, what it is you do. – *I praise.*
How can you look into the monster's gaze
And accept what has death in it? – *I praise.*
But, poet, the anonymous and those
With no name, how do you call on them? – *I praise.*
What right have you though, in each changed disguise,
In each new mask, to trust your truth? – *I praise.*
Both calm and violent things know you for theirs,
Both star and storm: how so? *Because I praise.*

Notes

The Invalid Storyteller, p.17.   This was originally a narrative sequence in five parts. It is spoken by a group of unnamed people who, as children, paid regular visits to an old man on his sickbed. The old man told them stories with a tragic inflection to them. At the end of the sequence, he dies.

Sanctuary, p.31.   When the Huns and the Lombards invaded Northern Italy, the Veneti sought refuge on the islands of their lagoon. One of these islands, Torcello, was their commercial centre up until the foundation of the city of Venice. The islands were constantly vulnerable to attack – both from the Lombards on the mainland and from the Barbary pirates at sea.

The Disenchanted, p.32.   Grimshaw's painting is in the Tate Gallery, London.

Saxon Buckle, p.34.   The Sutton Hoo treasure is in the British Museum. The great gold belt-buckle dates from the seventh century.

On the Demolition of the 'Kite' District, p.38.   The Kite is a modest residential district of central Cambridge which suffered from planning blight for a number of years. Much of it was finally demolished in the spring of 1980.

On the Devil's Dyke, p.46.   The dyke is a large earthwork, about 7½ miles in length, near the Cambridgeshire-Suffolk border. It is thought to have been built to defend the kingdom of East Anglia against incursions along the Icknield Way.

The Natural History of the Rook, p.49, includes quotations from Charles Waterton's *Essays on Natural History*. Waterton (1782-1865) turned his estate at Walton Hall, Yorkshire, into the world's first wild-life sanctuary.

To Nicholas Hawksmoor, p.56.   All Souls is the Oxford College, but Christ Church is the parish church of Spitalfields in the East End of London.

The Peaceable Kingdom, p.60.   In the Golden Age, wrote Fulke Greville, 'The laws were inward that did rule the heart' (*Caelica* XLIV).

A Prayer for my Children, p.62, is loosely based on the sixth century Evening Hymn, 'Te lucis ante terminum'. (See *The Penguin Book of Latin Verse*, p.113.)

Invocation, p.65, and *Two Versions of Caedmon*, p.66.   The Venerable Bede in his *Ecclesiastical History of the English People* tells the story of the poet Caedmon, who was a herdsman at the abbey of Whitby in the seventh century. According to Bede, Caedmon would slip out of hall after dinner to avoid being called upon to sing at table. One night, when he was sleeping with the cattle, an angel appeared to him in a dream and told him to sing of how God made the world. This is the origin, Bede tells us, of the nine-line poem known as Caedmon's Hymn, the earliest poem by a known author in any dialect of English. Bede quotes the poem in a Latin prose version, though the original Northumbrian survives, as does a translation into Wessex dialect. I have used all three texts for my 'Two Versions'.

Three Brueghel Paintings, p.67   In the Kunsthistorisches Museum, Vienna.

The San Damiano Crucifix, p.69.   In St Bonaventura's *Life of St Francis*, we learn how St Francis embarked on his ministry. As he knelt in prayer in the ruined church of San Damiano, he heard a voice from the painted crucifix over the altar. 'Francis,' it said, 'go and repair My House, which, as thou seest, is falling utterly into ruin.' Soon afterwards the Saint began the task of rebuilding what Bonaventura calls 'the material church'.

The Infinite Variety, p.73.   The Moghul Emperor, Shah Jahan, was a patron of miniature painting.

Work, p.82.   The sculpture described in Part 2 is in the Chapter House of Southwell Minster, Nottinghamshire.

The Law of the House, p.84.   The title translates the Greek word *oikonomia*, from which our word 'economy' derives. The first line is from Pound's Canto XLV: 'With usura hath no man a house of good stone'.

At the Grave of William Morris, p.86   Morris's grave was designed by his friend, the architect Philip Webb, in imitation of an Icelandic tomb. It is shaped like a gabled roof. Morris, incidentally, was an atheist.

Lindisfarne Sacked, p.112.   The Northumbrian abbey of Lindisfarne on Holy Island was sacked by the Vikings in 793. The magnificent Lindisfarne Gospels, made in the abbey at the end of the previous century, were somehow spirited away to the mainland and so preserved. Many other manuscripts of the same school, however, must have perished in the flames.

Kaspar Hauser, p.114.   In 1828, a sixteen-year-old youth was found wandering in the streets of Nuremberg. He was only able to speak a single sentence: 'I want to be a horseman like my father.' When he was taken in by the local pastor and taught more language, it emerged that he had been kept in a dark room, possibly a stable, for as long as he could remember and had never encountered human society before. He had no idea who had been looking after him. In 1833 he died a violent death: it is normally assumed that he was murdered, though he may have committed suicide.

The Keeper of Flocks and *You who, believing in your Christs and Marys*, pp.123-5.   Many of Pessoa's poems purport to have been written by 'heteronyms': characters he invented as a way of presenting attitudes of mind that preoccupied him or significantly contrasted with his own. They were also a way of escaping from his own personality. 'Alberto Caeiro' and 'Ricardo Reis' are both neo-pagans, though there their similarity ends. Caeiro is an uneducated peasant, Reis a sophisticated doctor.

A Mountain Garden, *Forced March* and *Postcard*, pp.125-127.
The dates following these poems are Radnóti's. From 1940 onwards, Radnóti was a conscript in various forced labour battalions. In 1944, when he was encamped in Serbia, he and his fellow-labourers were force-marched back across Hungary. *Forced March* and *Postcard* were written as they went, the latter only a month before his death by firing-squad.

To Imre Nagy, p.129.   Nagy was Prime Minister of Hungary from October to November 1956. His was the reformist government that briefly attempted to resist Soviet power in Hungary. The poem alludes to the evening before the Soviet invasion when Nagy, on the point of taking office, sought unsuccessfully to calm his supporters in the street outside Parliament. In 1958 he was tried *in camera* and hanged in a prison yard on the outskirts of Budapest.

Daydreams, p.129.   *Sors bona nihil aliud*: a well-known motto meaning roughly 'Good fortune or nothing'.